Everyday
GOURMET
Cookbook

Cover image and all photography © Kaycee Leishman

Cover design copyright © 2013 by Covenant Communications, Inc.
Cover and Interior designed by Christina Marcano

Published by Covenant Communications, Inc.
American Fork, Utah

Printed in China
First Printing: October 2013

19 18 17 16 15 14 13   10 9 8 7 6 5 4 3 2 1

ISBN 978-1-62108-472-3

Everyday
GOURMET
Cookbook

Introduction

A *gourmet* is one who appreciates and prepares superb food. Wouldn't we all want to be considered gourmets? But wait—when you hear *gourmet*, you probably think complicated recipes, expensive ingredients, and time-consuming processes.

If so, think again!

You're in for a pleasant surprise. It is possible to prepare superb food without all the complexity, cost, and hours so many typical "gourmet" recipes require.

In *Everyday Gourmet* we've added special touches to tried-and-true recipes—new twists on familiar themes that move our recipes to "gourmet" status. You'll appreciate how easy (we include step-by-step tutoring) and affordable (we build dishes around common pantry staples) these unique recipes are. And those you cook for will appreciate how beautiful your dishes look and how delicious everything tastes.

Because gourmet cooks understand that we eat with our eyes before we ever taste a bite, we also include suggestions and ideas on attractive ways to present many of these dishes. And because we believe we're more inclined to do things that are easy, we've included tips for working smarter instead of harder in the kitchen.

Superb is always possible! By using ingredients in unusual combinations and serving dishes in pretty ways, we provide inspiring, mouth-watering, and crowd-pleasing recipes that will move you and your cooking over to gourmet status. We celebrate the appreciation and preparation of superb food and invite you to join us in becoming gourmets—everyday gourmets!

— *Alice Osborne, Jeanne Wolfley, and Kaycee Leishman*

Table of Contents

Appetizers

An appetizer is anything that excites the appetite or provides relish. Traditionally appetizers are sweet or savory bits of food served before a meal—a menu of beautiful finger foods often used especially for entertaining. While appetizers can make a great snack, they can be so hearty and satisfying that you'll often hear those gathered around the serving table say that they could make an entire meal out of them. Fresh ingredients and creative presentation make these dishes an exciting introduction to any meal or festive gathering.

Garden-Fresh Bruschetta

Yield: 12 servings | **Prep Time:** 15 minutes | **Cook Time:** 8 minutes

While dried basil can be substituted, fresh is always best and adds a special zing to this traditional recipe.

6 Roma tomatoes, chopped
½ cup sun-dried tomatoes, packed in olive oil
4 garlic cloves, minced
⅓ cup extra-virgin olive oil
2 tablespoons balsamic vinegar
¼ cup fresh basil, stems removed (packed)
¼ teaspoon salt
¼ teaspoon freshly ground black pepper
1 French baguette
2 cups shredded mozzarella cheese

Preheat oven to the broiler setting. In a large bowl, combine the Roma tomatoes, sun-dried tomatoes, garlic, olive oil, vinegar, basil, salt, and pepper. Allow the mixture to sit for 10 minutes.

Cut the baguette into ¾-inch slices. On a baking sheet, arrange the baguette slices in a single layer. Sprinkle baguette slices with mozzarella and then top with tomato mixture. Broil for 3–5 minutes, or until cheese is melted and bubbly. Watch closely so it doesn't burn.

Chicken Croquettes

Yield: 16–18 large croquettes | **Prep Time:** 10 minutes |
Chill Time: 1–2 hours | **Frying Time:** 2 minutes

Croquettes are a perfect way to use leftover chicken (you could also use turkey) and mashed potatoes. You can even freeze them for later use before breading. To serve them, just thaw the prepared balls, bread, and cook. And, of course, these are delicious paired with leftover gravy!

2 cups finely minced cooked chicken
1 cup seasoned mashed potatoes
2 tablespoons finely chopped fresh parsley (you can also use dried parsley)
1½ teaspoons black pepper

SAUCE

2 tablespoons butter
6 green onions (include a few inches of green shoots), thinly sliced
2 cloves garlic, finely minced (garlic may be omitted if using garlic mashed potatoes)
4 tablespoons flour
¼ cup chicken broth
¼ cup milk
½ teaspoon salt, or to taste

BREADING

½ cup flour
2 large eggs, lightly beaten with 1 tablespoon cold water
2 cups Italian-spiced Panko crumbs
Canola oil for frying

In a large bowl, combine chicken, mashed potatoes, parsley, and pepper. Set aside.

To prepare sauce: In a medium saucepan, melt butter over medium heat. Add green onions and garlic; cook, stirring for 1 minute. Add flour and stir until well blended. Stir in chicken broth and milk; continue cooking, stirring for another 2 minutes. Add salt to taste. This mixture will thicken. Combine sauce and chicken mixture; blend well. Cover and refrigerate until thoroughly chilled, approximately 1–2 hours.

To prepare breading: Sprinkle ½ cup flour on large plate. In a medium bowl, place beaten egg and water. In a separate medium bowl, put Panko crumbs. Shape chicken mixture into 1½-inch to 2-inch balls. Roll gently in the flour to coat, then roll in the egg mixture. Finally, roll in the Panko crumbs. Place on a foil-lined cookie sheet. Heat canola oil to 350°–360° F. Fry croquettes in small batches for approximately 2 minutes or until golden brown. Drain on paper towels. Serve with leftover gravy if desired.

Hummus with Tahini

Yield: 3 cups | **Prep Time:** 5 minutes | **Cooling Time:** 3 hours

There are two keys to brag-worthy hummus: First, let the flavor of the garbanzo beans (also known as chickpeas) come through. And second, use a light hand when adding lemon. Because of its fiber and high vitamin content, this healthy spread is a real favorite for snacking.

2½ cups canned garbanzo beans, drained and rinsed
¼–⅓ cup freshly squeezed lemon juice
⅓ cup tahini
2 cloves garlic, crushed
1–2 tablespoons extra-virgin olive oil
½ teaspoon ground cumin
Pinch of freshly ground black pepper
1 teaspoon kosher salt
⅓ cup water
Parsley, for garnish

Put all ingredients except the garbanzo beans and parsley into a blender; blend for 5 seconds. Add the beans and parsley. Blend on high until mixture reaches the consistency of a granular sour cream, approximately 10–15 seconds. If the hummus is too thick, slowly add a little water and blend until it reaches the desired consistency.

Transfer to a serving bowl; cover and refrigerate for a few hours before serving. The flavors will mingle well if given a chance to sit for a while. Serve with pita wedges, crackers, or slices of toasted whole-grain bread.

TIP: Thoroughly rinse the garbanzo beans to clear away the taste of any ingredients used in the canning process.

Smoked Salmon on Corn Cakes

Yield: 8 servings | **Prep Time:** 10 minutes | **Cook Time:** 5 minutes

Whole-kernel corn paired with smoked salmon is a delicious and surprising taste combination. Served with a fresh salad and crusty roll, this dish could easily become a main dinner course.

1 cup flour
1½ teaspoons baking powder
⅛ teaspoon cayenne pepper
½ teaspoon salt
¼ teaspoon freshly ground black pepper
2 large eggs, lightly beaten
1 cup milk
2 tablespoons butter, melted
1 cup fresh or frozen corn kernels
3 tablespoons extra-virgin olive oil, divided
8 small strips smoked salmon (approximately ½ pound)

In a medium bowl, sift the flour, baking powder, cayenne pepper, and salt. Add the freshly ground pepper. Gently stir in eggs and milk. Add melted butter and corn kernels; stir to make a batter but don't over-mix.

Preheat oven to warm. Heat 2 tablespoons olive oil in large nonstick skillet. Fry 4 corncakes: For each corncake, drop ¼ cup batter into the heated oil and spread to create a 4-inch round. Cook on medium heat until golden brown, approximately 5 minutes. Transfer cakes to a baking sheet and place in a warmed oven. Repeat process by adding remaining tablespoon of olive oil, if needed, to skillet; when oil is heated, add remaining batter to cook 4 more corncake rounds.

To serve, top each corncake with smoked salmon strips and arrange on serving tray or platter.

Zesty Garden Salsa

Yield: 4 cups | **Prep Time:** 10 minutes

This different twist on traditional salsa is delicious served atop small Romaine lettuce leaves.

3 chopped Roma tomatoes
3 tablespoons chopped cilantro
½ cup chopped green onion
1 15-ounce can black-eyed peas with juice
1 15-ounce can corn, drained
¼ cup vinegar
1 1.34-ounce package Italian dressing seasoning
2 medium avocados, diced

In a medium bowl, mix all ingredients except avocados; refrigerate. Prepare and add avocados just before serving.

Chicken Lettuce Wraps

Yield: 2–3 servings | **Prep Time:** 25 minutes

Taking on the challenge of coming up with our own version of restaurant-style lettuce wraps led us to a recipe that you can now confidently make in the comfort of your own kitchen!

SPECIAL SAUCE

¼ cup sugar
½ cup water
2 tablespoons soy sauce
2 tablespoons rice wine vinegar
2 tablespoons ketchup
2 tablespoons lemon juice
½ teaspoon sesame oil
2 teaspoons Dijon mustard
2 teaspoons hot water
1 teaspoon minced garlic
1 teaspoon chili sauce

CHICKEN

¼ cup extra-virgin olive oil, divided
2 boneless, skinless chicken breasts
1 cup water chestnuts
1 cup mushrooms
½ cup thinly sliced carrots

STIR-FRY SAUCE

6 tablespoons soy sauce
¼ cup brown sugar
1 teaspoon rice wine vinegar
2 teaspoons minced garlic
3 tablespoons chopped shallots
4–5 leaves iceberg lettuce

To prepare special sauce: In a small bowl, dissolve ¼ cup sugar in ½ cup water. Add soy sauce, vinegar, ketchup, lemon juice, and sesame oil. Mix well and refrigerate sauce until you're ready to serve lettuce wraps. Combine mustard with hot water. Before serving the sauce, add the mustard-flavored water, minced garlic, and chili sauce to taste.

To prepare chicken: Bring 3 tablespoons olive oil to high heat in a wok or large frying pan. Sauté chicken breasts

for 4–5 minutes per side or until cooked through and juices run clear. Remove chicken from pan and cool. Keep oil in the pan; keep hot.

As chicken cools, mince water chestnuts and mushrooms to approximately the size of small peas. When chicken is cool, mince it to approximately the size of small peas.

To make stir-fry sauce: In a small bowl, mix soy sauce, brown sugar, and rice vinegar together. With the pan on high heat, add 1 tablespoon of olive oil. Add chicken, garlic, shallots, water chestnuts, and mushrooms. Add the stir-fry sauce and sauté mixture for 2 minutes. Spoon the chicken mixture into lettuce leaves. Wrap tightly and place wrap, seam side down, on serving plate. Top each wrap with special sauce. Serve immediately.

Dill and Yogurt Dip

Yield: 4 servings | **Prep Time:** 10 minutes

Your mama always told you to eat your veggies. Make it easy and make her proud with a tasty dip and swoon-worthy presentation.

1 large head red cabbage
12 ounces plain Greek yogurt
⅓ cup diced red pepper
¼ cup thinly sliced green onions
1 cup finely chopped broccoli florets
2 tablespoons dried dill
¼ teaspoon garlic salt

Cut off just enough of the cabbage bottom so it sits flat on a serving plate. Pull several outside leaves back; leave enough to create the outsides of a bowl. Scoop out the insides of the cabbage with a sharp ice cream scoop, being careful not to cut too far into the edges or bottom of the cabbage.

In a medium bowl, combine the remaining ingredients. Transfer the completed dip to the red cabbage bowl. Serve with crudités and crackers.

Overstuffed Tomatoes

Yield: 4 servings | **Prep Time:** 15 minutes | **Chill Time:** 1 hour

This hearty dish is both easy to make and easy on the waistline. It's also an excellent way to use leftover grilled salmon. Lovely to look at and very tasty, this is truly a gourmet approach to serving a unique appetizer.

4 large tomatoes (at least 3 inches in diameter), room temperature
3 2.5-ounce foil packages salmon or 1 cup leftover grilled salmon
½ cup coarse bread crumbs
¼ cup chopped red onion
½ cup shredded Asiago cheese
½ cup mayonnaise
¼ cup chopped celery
2 teaspoons capers
Juice of 1 lemon (approximately 3 tablespoons)
⅛ teaspoon salt
⅛ teaspoon black pepper
Fresh dill sprigs (can also use dried dill)

Slice ½ inch off tops of each tomato and dice top slices. Remove pulp from tomatoes, leaving a "tomato cup"; discard seeds and dice the pulp flesh. Add diced tomato tops. In a large bowl, mix diced tomato and all other ingredients except salt, pepper, and tomato cups. Refrigerate for at least an hour to allow flavors to blend. Salt and pepper interiors of each tomato cup and fill with salmon mixture. Garnish tops with fresh dill sprigs or dried dill. Serve immediately.

Breads, Rolls, and Muffins

Don't you love to bake? There's something about using your hands—baking from scratch—that is so satisfying. And the aroma of baked goods calls up great memories and creates such a cozy ambience in a home.

Our mantra is, "Food tastes better made with butter and love!" so you'll see most of our recipes call for butter. Just think—just combine glorious butter with this white powdery stuff (also known as flour), stir in a few more ingredients, and you end up with breads, rolls, and muffins that will not only satisfy your creativity but will make others happy as well!

Tomato Bread

Yield: 2 loaves | **Prep Time:** 20 minutes | **Rise Time:** 1½ hours
Bake Time: 35–40 minutes

This exceptional gourmet bread makes amazing toasted cheese and BLT sandwiches, thanks to the full-bodied flavor of the tomatoes and herbs.

8 Roma tomatoes, quartered (or an 8-ounce can of tomato sauce plus 1 cup water)
¼ cup water
2 tablespoons extra-virgin olive oil
6–6½ cups flour, divided
3 tablespoons sugar
2 tablespoons active dry yeast
¾ teaspoon dried oregano
½ teaspoon garlic powder
½ teaspoon dried basil
1 teaspoon salt
½ cup grated Parmesan cheese

In a medium saucepan, cook tomatoes in water until soft; using a blender or food processor, purée tomatoes. Let cool. (If using canned tomato sauce, combine tomato sauce and water; heat then let cool.)

In a large mixing bowl, combine tomato mixture, olive oil, 3 cups flour, sugar, yeast, oregano, garlic powder, basil, and salt. Beat until smooth. Add Parmesan cheese and remaining flour to make a soft dough. Knead for 8 minutes. Place dough in a well-oiled, large bowl, turning dough once to oil its top. Cover and let rise in a warm place until doubled, approximately 1 hour.

Preheat oven to 350° F. Punch dough down. Turn onto lightly floured surface; divide dough in half. Shape into 2 loaves. Place dough into 2 well-oiled 8 x 4 x 2-inch bread pans. Cover and let rise until doubled, approximately 30 minutes. Bake for 35–40 minutes or until bread is lightly browned. Remove from pans and cool on a wire rack.

Breadsticks

Yield: 32 large breadsticks | **Prep Time:** 2 hours
Total Time: 2 hours 15 minutes

This recipe can easily be halved, but why not make them all and freeze the rest for another day?

2 tablespoons rapid-rise yeast (such as
    Instant SAF)
2 tablespoons sugar
1 tablespoon salt
7½–8 cups flour
2 teaspoons garlic salt
¼ cup extra-virgin olive oil
3 cups hot water
½ cup butter, melted

Preheat oven to warm for 3 or 4 minutes. Turn oven off. In large mixing bowl, add all dry ingredients (including the yeast); mix thoroughly. Add olive oil and hot water; blend well. Knead dough for 10 minutes to develop the gluten fibers. Place dough in large, greased bowl; cover and let dough rise in prewarmed oven until double, approximately 1 hour.

Punch dough down; divide dough in half. On a floured surface, roll half of the dough into a 12- x 18-inch rectangle. Brush with melted butter. Cut dough in half vertically, and then in half horizontally into 8 strips (making 16 breadsticks from half of the dough). Repeat this same step with the other half of the dough, creating 32 breadsticks total. Preheat oven to 350° F and try any of these variations:

Twists: Butter 32 10-inch wooden dowels (⅛ to ¼ inch); twist one piece of breadstick dough around each skewer. Lay skewers across rimmed cookie sheet. Let rise 10 minutes. Bake for 15–18 minutes at 350° F.

Cheesy Sticks: Butter breadstick dough and press buttered side down into freshly grated Parmesan or Romano cheese. Place buttered and cheesed sticks on oiled, parchment-lined baking sheet. Let rise 10 minutes. Bake for 15–18 minutes at 350° F.

Herb and Cheese Sticks: Spread melted butter on pieces of breadstick dough; sprinkle with Parmesan or Romano

cheese and Salad Supreme. Place breadsticks on oiled baking sheets and let rise 10 minutes. Bake for 15–18 minutes at 350° F. Brush with remaining melted butter after baking.

Pizza Sticks: Butter breadsticks and place on oiled baking sheet. Allow to rise 10 minutes. Spread dough with pizza sauce and place small pieces of pepperoni atop sauce. Bake for 15–18 minutes at 350° F; sprinkle with shredded cheese during the last 5 minutes of baking.

Cinnamon Sugar Sticks: Dip each piece of breadstick dough in melted butter. Roll sticks in mixture of 2 cups brown sugar and approximately 1 tablespoon cinnamon (to taste). Twist sticks and let rise on buttered, parchment-lined baking sheets. Let rise 10 minutes. Bake for 15–18 minutes at 350° F.

Artisan Crust Bread

Yield: 1 loaf | **Prep Time:** 5 minutes | **Rising Time:** 12–18 hours
Bake Time: 1 hour

Artisan bread is a creative endeavor that welcomes experimentation with tasty add-ins such as herbs or various cheeses. It is traditionally made in a clay pot with a lid and lots of love. This easy recipe involves a little chemistry and three basic steps.

1. The water measurement must be exact.
2. The oven, pot, and lid must be "screaming hot" before adding the dough and baking.
3. This bread must bake for an entire hour for the loaf to be completely baked inside the thick crust.

3 cups flour
¼ teaspoon active dry yeast
1¾–2 teaspoons salt (to taste)
1½ cups plus 2 tablespoons water, room temperature
Additional flour or cornmeal for dusting

In a large bowl, combine flour, yeast, and salt. If you are making a cheese or herbed bread, add these ingredients to the dry ingredients. Stir in water until blended. The dough will be lumpy and sticky; do not knead it. Cover with plastic wrap or a lid. Set dough aside—on a counter top or in the pantry, away from light—for 12–18 hours. The dough will get spongy as it sits.

When ready to bake, preheat your oven, pot, and lid to 500° F for 20–30 minutes. The pot and lid can be cast iron, clay, or anything else that conducts heat well.

Meanwhile, evenly sprinkle flour or cornmeal (approximately ¼ cup) over a flour sack or tea towel (do NOT use terrycloth). Cover one half of the towel with dough and quickly shape it into a flat ball (shape isn't crucial, as this is a rustic bread). Place the other half of the floured towel atop the bread ball. Let dough rest for 15–20 minutes. When ready to bake, reduce oven heat to 375° F. Remove pot and lid from oven. Carefully place dough in pot; don't worry about what it looks like. Shake pot to center the dough.

Bake for 1 hour at 375–400° F; due to varying oven temperatures, you will need to experiment with your oven. Check after 45 minutes; if the bread isn't as brown as you'd like, let it bake for the last 10–15 minutes without the lid. Just be sure your bread bakes for 1 full hour, as it will look done before it actually is. When baking is complete, turn loaf onto a wire rack and let cool.

NOTE: There is deliberately no oil in the bread or pan. Whole-wheat flour will not work with this recipe.

Cookie Dough Sweet Rolls

Yield: 24 large rolls | **Prep Time:** 40 minutes | **Bake Time:** 20 minutes

Our special twist on a familiar favorite—a cookie-type filling—makes these one of the most-asked-for treats in our families! This delectable combination of soft rolls and gooey cookie dough is a perfect treat that satisfies both the sweet roll lover and the cookie lover in one fell swoop!

STEP 1: COOKIE CRUMBLE FILLING

1 cup butter
2 cups brown sugar
2 eggs
3 cups oatmeal
2½ cups flour
2 teaspoons vanilla extract
1 teaspoon baking soda
1 teaspoon salt

In a large bowl, cream butter and brown sugar. Add eggs and mix until fluffy. Stir in remaining ingredients and set aside as you complete STEP 2.

STEP 2: ROLL DOUGH

2⅓ cups warm water
4 tablespoons active dry yeast
½ cup sugar
⅔ cup canola oil

In a large bowl, whisk water, yeast, sugar, and oil; let rest for 15 minutes. While the yeast mixture is resting, complete STEP 3.

STEP 3: CHOCOLATE SPREAD

1 14-ounce can sweetened condensed milk
1 12-ounce package chocolate chips
2 teaspoons vanilla extract
½ teaspoon salt

In a medium saucepan, combine all ingredients; cook over medium heat until ingredients are melted and incorporated well. Move on to STEP 4.

STEP 4: FINISH ROLL DOUGH

2 eggs
7 cups flour
2 teaspoons salt

Preheat oven to 350°F. Spray two 12-cup muffin tins well with nonstick cooking spray. To previously prepared yeast mixture,

add eggs 1 at a time; stir well after each addition. Add flour, 1 cup at a time; stir well after each addition. Add salt; mix by hand just until ingredients are fully incorporated.

On floured surface, roll dough into two separate rectangles; cover each rectangle with Chocolate Spread. Sprinkle Cookie Crumble Filling over chocolate layer. Roll each rectangle into tight logs. Using dental floss or string, cut rolls ½ inch thick.

Place rolls in prepared muffin cups; let raise 15 minutes. Bake for 20 minutes or until golden brown and not doughy in the middle. Place rolls on wire rack. While rolls are still warm, complete STEP 5.

STEP 5: FROSTING
½ cup butter, softened
2 teaspoons vanilla extract
3 cups powdered sugar
4 tablespoons milk

Blend all ingredients until smooth and creamy. Frost rolls while still warm.

Cheesy Cornbread Rounds

Yield: 9 servings | **Prep Time:** 15 minutes | **Bake Time:** 40 minutes

Cheese and buttermilk add a gourmet touch that gives this mealtime mainstay a special flavor and pleasant texture. Cutting the bread in rounds, rather than the traditional squares, is an unusual and eye-catching way to serve this satisfying dish.

½ cup butter, softened
⅔ cup sugar
2 eggs
1 cup buttermilk
½ teaspoon baking soda
1 cup cornmeal
1 cup flour
1 cup finely grated Cheddar cheese
¾ teaspoon salt

Preheat oven to 350° F. Grease an 8-inch square pan. In a large skillet, melt butter; remove from heat and stir in sugar. Quickly add eggs and beat until well blended. In a small bowl, combine buttermilk and baking soda; add to mixture in the skillet. Stir in cornmeal, flour, cheese, and salt until blended; a few lumps should remain. Pour batter into prepared baking pan. Bake 30–40 minutes, or until a toothpick inserted into the center comes out clean.

Macadamia Nut White Chocolate Muffins

Yield: 12 muffins | **Prep Time:** 15 minutes | **Bake Time:** 30–35 minutes

For vanilla lovers, a great big white-on-white hunk of cake disguised as a muffin! What a lovely addition to the brunch table.

½ cup butter, softened
¾ cup sugar
2 eggs
1 tablespoon vanilla extract
1 cup half-and-half
1½ cups flour
½ cup plus 2 tablespoons cake flour*
1 tablespoon baking powder
¼ teaspoon salt
¾ cup macadamia nuts, chopped and toasted*
¾ cup white chocolate chips

Preheat oven to 350° F. Grease a 12-cup muffin tin or line with paper cups. In a medium bowl, cream butter until fluffy. Slowly add sugar, continuing to beat. Add eggs, one at a time, beating well after each. Add vanilla and half-and-half. Beat until evenly blended.

In a large bowl, sift both flours, baking powder, and salt. Add white chocolate chips and nuts; mix well. Gently fold into half-and-half mixture; mix just until flour disappears. Fill muffin cups with batter until ¾ full. Bake 30–35 minutes or until slightly golden on the edges and a toothpick inserted into the middle of muffin comes out clean.

*Cake Flour: There's no need to run out and purchase cake flour just for this recipe. Make your own, using all-purpose flour and cornstarch. To make your own cake flour, replace 2 tablespoons of all-purpose flour with 2 tablespoons of cornstarch. For this recipe, since you want ½ cup plus 2 tablespoons cake flour, measure ½ cup all-purpose flour and 2 tablespoons cornstarch into a sifter. Sift these 2 ingredients together well and then proceed with the recipe as instructed.

*Toasted Nuts: Toasting nuts is a step some cooks skip, which is unfortunate—this simple effort can really bump a recipe from okay to gourmet! Toasting nuts deepens their flavor (making them even more nutty and complex) and also gives them a crunchy texture, which is one of the reasons we add nuts to our food.

It is important to check the nuts and stir them often while they're toasting. You'll notice that nuts on the edges of the pan start to brown sooner than the nuts in the middle, and because most ovens have hot spots, it's necessary to move the nuts around for even roasting.

Preheat oven to 350° F. Spread nuts in an even layer on a baking sheet. You can use a cake tin for smaller amounts, as the higher sides will allow you to shake the pan for even distribution. Toast in the oven for approximately 3 minutes or until nuts start to turn golden. Remove during toasting and move the nuts around. They'll have a nutty aroma, and you might hear some crackling. Return to the oven if needed and check again after another 3 minutes. When they've reached the desired color, remove and cool on another tray or plate—cooling them on the sheet they were toasted on risks continued cooking and scorching.

If the recipe calls for chopped nuts, chop them after you roast them. It is very easy to burn chopped nuts because the pieces are so small. Warm nuts also chop more cleanly and with less flaking.

Traditional English Scones

Yield: 8 scones | **Prep Time:** 10 minutes | **Bake Time:** 15–20 minutes

The traditional English scone is baked, not fried, and is light, fluffy, and scrumptious. This easy recipe is destined to become a breakfast or brunch favorite!

1¾ cups flour
2 teaspoons baking powder
½ teaspoon salt
3 tablespoons sugar, divided
8 tablespoons cold butter, cut into ½-inch cubes
½ cup dried cranberries
½ cup white chocolate chips
¾ cup buttermilk, divided

Preheat oven to 400° F. Using an electric mixer, combine flour, baking powder, salt, and 1 tablespoon sugar. Add the cold butter and mix just until butter is coated with flour (butter chunks should remain fairly large). Add cranberries and white chocolate chips. Stir gently. Add in ⅔ cup buttermilk. Stop mixing when dough begins to pull away from the sides of the bowl. Quickly shape dough into a ball and pat into a circle about ½ inch thick. Cut into 8 pie-shaped wedges. Place wedges on a baking sheet lined with parchment paper. Brush tops with remaining buttermilk and sprinkle generously with the remaining 2 tablespoons of sugar. Bake 15–20 minutes.

TIPS FOR AMAZING SCONES:
All equipment and ingredients, including your hands, should be as cool as possible. Butter should be very cold, but not frozen. If hands, ingredients, and equipment are too warm, they will melt the butter into the dough, resulting in heavy scones. The goal is for the butter to be gently rubbed in.

Work as quickly and as lightly as you can. Avoid over-rubbing or over-kneading the scone mixture. It will not be super-smooth; you want a light, pliable dough.

When cutting the dough, use a sharp knife. A blunt knife will tear at the edges of the scone and stunt its rise.

Bake near the top of the oven; scones like it best near the top.

Quick Crescent Rolls

Yield: 24 rolls | **Prep Time:** 20 minutes | **Rise Time:** 3–5 hours
Bake Time: 15 minutes

These no-fail, quick, and easy rolls freeze well. What could be smarter than always having ready-to-bake homemade rolls on hand?

1 cup warm water
1 tablespoon active dry yeast
¼ cup plus ½ teaspoon sugar, divided
4½–5 cups flour
2 teaspoons salt
2 eggs, slightly beaten
½ cup butter, softened and divided
1 cup milk

Pour the water into a large mixing bowl or stand mixer; stir in the yeast and ½ teaspoon sugar. Let the mixture sit for 5 minutes, or until it starts to bubble. Add remaining ¼ cup sugar, 2 cups flour, salt, eggs, and 4 tablespoons softened butter. Mix dough for 1 minute.

In a saucepan, heat the milk on the stovetop or in the microwave until it starts to simmer; cool slightly and add to the dough. Add the remaining flour, 1 cup at a time, mixing well after each addition, until the dough pulls away from the sides of the bowl. Knead for 10 minutes by hand or in the stand mixer on medium speed for 5 minutes.

Place dough on a lightly oiled surface. Shape dough into an oval and let it rest for 5 minutes. Note: Make sure to let the dough rest so it will roll out easily. Roll the dough into a circle and spread the remaining butter over the top. Cut dough into quarters with a pizza cutter. Cut each quarter into thirds. Starting at the outside edge, roll each triangle in toward the center of the circle to form a standard crescent roll.

Line a baking sheet with parchment paper; coat paper well with cooking spray. Place each roll onto parchment. Cover loosely with buttered or oiled plastic wrap. You'll want the coated side of the wrap touching the rolls; wrap your pan securely. Place pan in freezer overnight or until rolls are solidly frozen. Place frozen rolls in freezer-safe bags for storage.

To bake: Preheat oven to 350° F. Place frozen rolls on a lightly oiled baking sheet, cover with oiled plastic wrap, and allow to rise for 3–5 hours or until the dough has risen approximately 1 inch above the rim of the pan. Note: The rolls will rise faster in a warm environment. Remove the plastic wrap and bake 15 minutes or until golden brown.

Variation: Butter Flake Rolls

Roll rested dough into a rectangle and spread with the remaining butter. Using a pizza cutter, slice dough into quarters and each quarter into thirds. Stack 4 strips on top of each other and cut the stacks into 2-inch-wide pieces. Freeze according to directions above. To bake Butter Flake Rolls, lay each stack on its side in a well-oiled muffin tin; let rise and bake at 400° F for 12 minutes. Remove rolls to cooling rack.

Sopapilla Fries

Yield: 12 servings | **Prep Time:** 2 hours | **Cook Time:** 2–5 minutes

Sopapilla is a kind of fried pastry—a type of quick bread that originated in several Latin American countries. This recipe eventually made its way to New Mexico and Texas, and its popularity has been spreading ever since. A delicious treat, it is traditionally made from leavened wheat dough to which some shortening or butter is added. After being allowed to rise, the dough is rolled into a sheet that is then cut into circular, square, or triangular shapes. They are then deep-fried in oil, sometimes after allowing them to rise further before frying; the frying causes the shapes to puff up, ideally forming a hollow pocket in the center.

Our twist on this popular theme is to cut the dough in small strips to make pretty little "fries." Whether you prepare fries or the traditional circles, squares, or triangles, rest assured they'll be a big hit!

¼ cup warm water
1 tablespoon active dry yeast
6 tablespoons sugar, divided
¾ cup milk
1 teaspoon salt
2 tablespoons butter
1 egg
3 cups flour

In a small bowl, add water, yeast, and 3 tablespoons sugar. Let yeast mixture sit and "proof" (grow) for 3–5 minutes.

In a medium saucepan, bring 3 remaining tablespoons sugar, milk, and salt to a boil. Remove pan from heat. Add butter and let mixture sit until lukewarm. In a small bowl, beat egg with a fork. Add 1 cup flour, beaten egg, and proofed yeast to milk mixture. Continue adding flour a little at a time, stirring after each addition, until all 3 cups have been added. Place dough in buttered bowl, cover with a damp cloth, and allow to rise until doubled in size, approximately 1½–2 hours.

Punch dough down; place on a lightly floured surface and knead for 3 minutes or until dough is smooth. Cover dough and allow to rest for 20 minutes. Roll dough to a ½-inch thick square; cut into strips, approximately 2 inches long by ⅛ inch wide. Heat oil to 350° F; fry a few fries at a time, turning fries until both sides are puffy and golden brown.

Drain on paper towels and sprinkle with powdered sugar and cinnamon.

TIP: These are also delicious served with a dip of thin vanilla glaze.

Wendell's Maple Bars & Glazed Doughnuts

Yield: 8–10 maple bars or donuts with holes | **Prep Time**: 2 hours | **Frying Time**: 2½–3 minutes

Hot, delicious, melt-in-your-mouth doughnuts are easier to make than you might think. This beloved recipe was the one Alice's father, Wendell, used in his doughnut shop—and Alice grew up "testing" his beautiful and delicious creations every day. Doughnuts are easily made via an assembly line of operations, so gather the family and set up your own doughnut-making event.

2 tablespoons active dry yeast
¼ cup warm water
¾ cup milk, scalded, then cooled
¼ cup sugar
1 teaspoon salt
1 egg
¼ cup butter, softened
3 cups sifted flour
Canola oil for frying (approximately 2 quarts)

In a mixing bowl, dissolve yeast in warm water. Add scalded milk, sugar, salt, egg, butter, and half the flour. Mix until smooth. Gradually add remaining flour until the dough is easy to handle. Turn onto a lightly floured surface and knead until smooth. Place dough in a large, well-buttered bowl; turn dough over so the top has a light covering of butter. Cover bowl with a damp, clean towel. Let rise in a warm place until doubled; punch down and roll dough out onto a floured surface to approximately 1 inch thick. Cut 4-inch rectangles for maple bars or cut rounds using a doughnut cutter. Let bars or doughnuts and holes rise until light, uncovered (so a crust will form), approximately 10 minutes.

Set the thermostat on a deep-sided electric frying pan to 360° F. When the oil reaches the right temperature, it will start to smoke. Drop bars or doughnuts into oil, 3 or 4 at a time, and fry 1½ minutes or until golden brown. Turn and cook approximately 1 more minute. Remove and drain on paper towels.

When cool enough to handle, dip each bar or doughnut in icing or glaze.

MAPLE ICING

3½ tablespoons whole milk or cream
½ teaspoon maple flavoring
2⅔ cups powdered sugar
2 tablespoons butter, softened

In a medium saucepan, heat milk and maple flavoring over low heat until warm. Sift sugar into milk mixture. Whisk slowly until well combined. Remove icing from heat and add butter. Mix well. Set icing over a bowl of warm water so it doesn't form a crust.

VANILLA GLAZE
¼ cup whole milk or cream
1 teaspoon vanilla extract
2 cups powdered sugar

In a medium saucepan, heat milk and vanilla over low heat until warm. Sift sugar into milk mixture. Whisk slowly until well combined. Remove glaze from heat and set over a bowl of warm water so it doesn't form a crust.

Breakfast and Brunch

Breakfast, the start to your day, is a golden opportunity to demonstrate to your family and friends how important they are. Few things say "I love you!" better than homemade food made from scratch. Here you'll find unique, easy, and amazing recipes perfect for any breakfast or celebratory brunch!

Thistle Inn Casserole

Yield: 6 servings | **Prep Time:** 10 minutes | **Bake Time:** 40–45 minutes

Gary and Pat Teske, retired keepers of the Thistle Inn in Holland, Michigan, served this award-winning breakfast casserole for several decades. It was a favorite with their guests and has become a favorite with our families and friends. This is a perfect make-ahead recipe that we like to serve at our neighborhood brunches—it keeps 'em coming back for more!

3 cups frozen, shredded hash brown potatoes
¾ cup shredded Monterey Jack cheese with jalapeño peppers or shredded sharp cheddar cheese
1 cup fully cooked, diced ham or Canadian bacon
¼ cup sliced green onion
4 beaten eggs
1 12-ounce can evaporated milk
¼ teaspoon pepper
⅛ teaspoon salt

Preheat oven to 350° F. Spray a 2-quart square baking dish with nonstick cooking spray. Arrange potatoes evenly in the bottom of the dish. Sprinkle with cheese, ham, and green onion.

In a medium mixing bowl, combine eggs, milk, pepper, and salt. Pour egg mixture over potato mixture in dish. (The dish may be covered and refrigerated at this point for several hours or overnight.)

Bake uncovered for 40–45 minutes (55–60 minutes if made ahead and chilled), or until center appears set. Let stand 5 minutes before serving. Garnish with diced fresh tomatoes or salsa.

Apple Cherry Pandowdy

Yield: 6 servings | **Prep Time:** 15 minutes | **Bake Time:** 35 minutes

This old-fashioned fruited dish would be perfect on a chilly fall morning.

BOTTOM CRUST

1 cup flour
2 teaspoons baking powder
½ teaspoon salt
1 cup milk
½ cup butter, melted

In a large bowl, mix flour, baking powder, salt, and milk. Stir in melted butter. Stir only until blended (be careful not to over-mix). Spoon batter into a well-buttered, 10-inch cast-iron skillet.

FRUIT LAYER

6 large apples, peeled, cored, and thinly
   sliced
¾ cup pecans
½ cup dried cherries
½ cup brown sugar
6 tablespoons butter, melted

Preheat oven to 350° F. Toss together apples, pecans, cherries, and brown sugar. Add melted butter. Spoon over batter and bake for 35 minutes. Serve with sweetened whipped cream or cream cheese topping (recipe follows).

CREAM CHEESE TOPPING

1 8-ounce package cream cheese, softened
2 tablespoons brown sugar
¼ cup milk

In a small bowl, mix all ingredients until smooth.

Apples and Brats Pancakes

Yield: 6–8 servings | **Prep Time:** 40 minutes total

This dish has been a consistent Father's Day brunch centerpiece—it's a man-pleasing dish for sure. It's also a wonderful addition to a camping menu—breakfast or otherwise.

APPLE AND BRATS TOPPING

1 package brats, sliced
½ cup apple juice
6 cups peeled, cored, and thinly sliced
    apples
1 tablespoon cinnamon
1 cup brown sugar

In a large frying pan, brown brats in apple juice. Stir in apples, cinnamon, and brown sugar. Cook together until meat is done and apples are soft. Serve hot over pancakes.

FLUFFIEST PANCAKES

1 cup flour
2 tablespoons sugar
2 tablespoons baking powder
½ teaspoon salt
2 tablespoons melted butter
1 large egg
1 cup buttermilk
2 tablespoons water

Sift all dry ingredients into a large bowl; create a well in the middle. In a separate small bowl, thoroughly mix butter, egg, and buttermilk. Pour liquid ingredients into the well in the dry ingredients. Mix lightly by hand using a spoon or rubber spatula. If batter is too thick, add 2 tablespoons water.

For large pancakes, pour ¼ cup batter per pancake onto a preheated griddle. Flip pancakes when edges look set, the wet shine is disappearing, and bubbles in the middle begin to pop. Cook an additional minute or until golden brown. Serve hot with Apples and Brats Topping.

NOTE: Buttermilk can come in various consistencies, from thick to thin, which can affect the consistency of your batter.

Everyday Gourmet Granola

Yield: Approximately 2 quarts–1 gallon | **Prep Time:** 30 minutes
Bake Time: 4 hours

Alice prepared a very basic version of this for her large family as a cost-cutting alternative to expensive and nutrient-empty boxed cold cereals. She has since made it "gourmet" with added ingredients. But the basic version is so good that it doesn't need any added attractions. The original was so basic that Alice dubbed it "Pauper's Granola"—but it was so good, she bagged it up and sold it at bazaars and fairs. The abundance of raves this granola has earned moved us to rename it "Everyday Gourmet Granola"!

BASIC VERSION

8 cups old-fashioned oats
1 cup powdered milk
1 cup whole-wheat flour
½ teaspoon salt
3 cups water
1 cup healthy oil (almond, sesame, coconut, olive)
1½ cups honey
1 cup brown sugar
2 cups old-fashioned peanut butter
3 tablespoons vanilla extract
4 cups raisins

Preheat oven to 210° F. In a large roasting pan, mix the dry ingredients. In a large saucepan over medium heat, combine the water, oil, honey, brown sugar, and peanut butter, stirring until peanut butter is dissolved and mixture is smooth. Remove from heat and stir in vanilla. Pour mixture over dry ingredients and mix well, being sure all ingredients are thoroughly coated.

Slow-roast granola for 4 hours or until it has turned golden brown, stirring every half hour or so to ensure even roasting. Remove from oven and mix in raisins. Allow granola to cool, then store in an airtight container for as long as 3 months. Will store in the refrigerator or freezer longer.

GOURMET VERSION

8 cups old-fashioned oats
1 cup powdered milk
1 cup whole-wheat flour
1 cup ground flaxseeds
1 cup ground chia seeds
1–2 cups sliced almonds (or other nuts, lightly chopped)
1 cup raw sunflower seeds

1 cup sesame seeds
1½ cups unsweetened shredded coconut
1 teaspoon salt
3½ cups water
1½ cups healthy oil (almond, sesame,
    coconut, olive)
2 cups honey
1 cup brown sugar
2½ cups old-fashioned peanut butter
3½ tablespoons vanilla extract
3 cups raisins

2 cups other dried and chopped fruit (such
    as cherries, cranberries, apricots,
    pineapple, and papaya)

Follow the same directions for mixing and
roasting as for the BASIC VERSION.

Leek Gratiné

Yield: 6–8 servings | **Prep Time:** 15 minutes | **Bake Time:** 25 minutes

A gratiné is quiche without the crust. It is traditionally made in a shallow-sided oval pan or dish, but a round or rectangular oven-safe dish works as well. The gratiné bakeware allows the food to cook evenly while the top browns nicely. For an impressive and tasty quiche-like entrée without the stress or added time of making a pie crust, gratiné is the way to go.

2 tablespoons butter, divided
6 slices bacon
8 medium-size leeks
½ cup water
4 eggs
1½ cups heavy cream
¼ teaspoon ground nutmeg
½ teaspoon salt
¼ teaspoon freshly ground black pepper, or
    to taste
½ cup grated sharp cheddar cheese
¼ cup grated Parmesan cheese

Preheat oven to 375° F. Using 1 tablespoon of the butter, lightly grease the baking dish. In a 10-inch skillet, brown bacon. While bacon is cooking, wash leeks well and slice into ½-inch rounds. When bacon has browned, remove most of the fat and add leeks and water to skillet. Cover and simmer leeks and bacon over low heat for 20 minutes or until leeks are tender and have absorbed the water. Evaporate any remaining water over medium heat, uncovered. Be sure to stir leeks occasionally while cooking to prevent burning.

Remove leeks and bacon to the bowl of a food processor or blender. Add eggs, cream, nutmeg, salt, and pepper. Process or blend for a few seconds at a time until the bacon is chopped. (Avoid over-processing; you want a chunky consistency, not a puree.) Pour the mixture into the prepared pie plate. Sprinkle grated cheeses and pieces of the remaining tablespoon of butter on top. Bake for 25 minutes or until the custard is set.

TIP: If the top begins to appear as if it will crack prior to completely baking through, spray or sprinkle several tablespoons of water on the walls of the hot oven to create steam, which will keep the top moist and prevent cracking.

Gourmet Pancake and Waffle Syrups

Yield: Approximately 1 quart per syrup | **Prep Time:** 5 minutes per syrup
Cook Time: 5 minutes per syrup

Specially flavored syrups are an easy way to jazz up what can often be a ho-hum breakfast of pancakes or waffles. Who knew simple ingredients such as peanut butter, cinnamon, buttermilk, or brown sugar could turn okay to gourmet?

PEANUT BUTTER SYRUP

2 cups brown sugar
1 cup water
1 cup peanut butter
1 teaspoon vanilla extract

In a medium saucepan, cook brown sugar and water over medium heat; bring syrup to a full boil then continue cooking for 2 minutes. Stir in peanut butter and continue cooking, stirring constantly, for 1 additional minute or until peanut butter is dissolved. Remove from heat and add vanilla.

CINNAMON SYRUP

2 cups sugar
½ cup water
1 cup corn syrup
2 teaspoons cinnamon
1 cup evaporated milk

In a medium saucepan, combine all ingredients except milk. Bring to a boil and cook for 2 minutes. Remove from heat and let stand 5 minutes; add milk and stir well.

BUTTERMILK SYRUP

1 cup butter
2 cups sugar
1 cup buttermilk
2 tablespoons corn syrup
1 teaspoon baking soda
2 teaspoons vanilla extract

In a large saucepan, combine butter, sugar, buttermilk, and corn syrup. Bring to a full boil and cook for 3 minutes. Remove from heat and add baking soda. The mixture will bubble up when you add the baking soda, so be sure you use a large pan. Stir in vanilla; blend well.

BUTTERMILK CARAMEL SYRUP

1½ cups buttermilk
1 cup sugar
1 cup brown sugar

½ cup butter
1 teaspoon baking soda
2 teaspoons vanilla

In a large saucepan over medium heat, combine buttermilk, sugar, brown sugar, and butter. Bring to a full boil; cook for 2 minutes. Remove from heat and add baking soda and vanilla. The mixture will bubble up when you add the baking soda, so be sure to use a large pan.

SYRUP NOTES:

—Most syrups thicken as they cool.
—Syrup does its best when served warm.
—Don't limit yourself to pancakes or waffles! Syrups can be used as topping for other foods, such as ice cream, spice cakes, pies, fruit crisps, cobblers, and even day-old Danishes and sweet rolls.

SO-Easy Quiche

Yield: 6 servings | **Prep Time:** 20 minutes | **Cook Time:** 40–45 minutes

This versatile recipe works well with any vegetables you have on hand. Packed with protein, it cuts calories and fat by using a rice crust—a clever way to use leftover rice—instead of traditional pie crust.

1 small zucchini, thinly sliced
5 slices bacon, precooked and chopped
1 Roma tomato, chopped
3 beaten eggs
½ cup grated cheese
¼ teaspoon pepper or seasoning of choice
Asparagus spears for garnish (optional)
Rice crust (recipe follows)

Preheat oven to 350° F. Place zucchini on the warm crust; add bacon and tomatoes. In a small bowl, mix eggs, cheese, and seasoning; pour over vegetables and bacon. If desired, top with asparagus spears. Bake for 40–45 minutes.

RICE CRUST

1½ cups cooked rice (white or brown)
¼ cup grated cheese
4 beaten eggs
¼ teaspoon dried dill
1 garlic clove, chopped

Preheat oven to 350° F. In a medium bowl, mix all ingredients; press into a buttered 8-inch pie plate. Bake for 15–20 minutes.

TIP: This quiche can be prepared the night before and kept covered in the refrigerator until ready to bake the next morning.

Fresh Blackberry Syrup Over Norwegian Waffles

Syrups make such a difference in the overall outcome of a pancake or waffle breakfast. Here fresh blackberries create a special stir—extra texture and visual eye appeal add to the excitement of biting into a traditional and hearty homemade favorite.

FRESH BLACKBERRY SYRUP
Yield: Approximately 3 cups | **Prep Time:** 30 minutes
Cook Time: 30 minutes

2 baskets fresh blackberries (or 16 ounces frozen blackberries), divided
1 cup sugar
2½ cups water, divided
½ teaspoon lemon juice
2 tablespoons cornstarch

Reserve ½ cup of the berries. In a large saucepan, place remaining berries, sugar, 2 cups water, and lemon juice; simmer for 25 minutes. In a small bowl, mix remaining ½ cup water and cornstarch until well blended; add to berries in pan. Stir constantly over low heat until berry mixture thickens. This recipe can be made ahead of time and reheated. When ready to serve, add reserved ½ cup berries to syrup; cook another 5 minutes or until added berries start to soften.

NORWEGIAN WAFFLES

Yield: 16 waffles |
Prep Time: 5 minutes |
Cook Time: 20–25 minutes

3 cups flour
3 teaspoons baking powder
½ teaspoon salt
4 tablespoons sugar
6 tablespoons butter, melted
3 cups milk
4 eggs

Preheat waffle iron. In a large bowl, combine dry ingredients. In a medium bowl, beat wet ingredients together. Add liquid mixture to dry ingredients and stir until just combined. Spray waffle iron with cooking spray, if necessary. Spoon batter onto waffle iron and cook until golden brown. Repeat with the remaining batter, keeping cooked waffles warm until serving.

Lunches

Lunch—for some, it's simply sustenance to get through the day; for others, it's the highlight of the day. It's with both sets of people in mind that we share these recipes. Whether you just want to grab a bite and get back to the work at hand, or you live for lunch and want to linger longer over a delectable dish, these nine alternatives to the typical peanut butter and jelly sandwich will work for you!

BBQ Chicken Pizza

Yield: 8 servings | **Prep Time:** 20 minutes plus standing
Bake Time: 25 minutes

Canned pizza crust turns this into a truly fast meal. Barbecue sauce, leftover chicken, vegetables, and cheese provide a flavor zing that pizza fans will rave about.

1 can refrigerator pizza crust dough (or you can make your own)
¼ cup barbecue sauce
½ cup marinara sauce
1½ cups cubed cooked chicken breast, divided
½ cup thinly sliced red onion
½ cup thinly sliced green pepper
1 clove garlic, minced
2 cups shredded mozzarella cheese

Preheat oven to 400° F. On a well-oiled surface, spread and roll dough out to form a large circle, approximately 14 inches. Transfer to a well-oiled pizza pan. Build up edges slightly. Combine the barbecue and marinara sauces and spread over the crust. Layer ¾ cup chicken, onion, bell pepper, garlic, and cheese. Repeat layers. Bake for 25–30 minutes or until pizza crust is golden brown.

TIPS: Bake or grill extra chicken with this meal in mind—cube and freeze for later pizza making. Also, it's fun to experiment with this recipe—so try other vegetables, such as sliced tomatoes, artichoke hearts, or diced green onions. Finally, don't hesitate to use that leftover holiday turkey—it is a superb partner with barbecue sauce!

Favorite Fajitas

Yield: 12 fajitas | **Prep Time:** 20 minutes | **Grilling Time:** 14–20 minutes

This delicious fajita can be cooked on the grill as well as the stovetop. It's easy to change the number of servings with this quick and pleasing recipe.

1 cup cilantro, chopped
1 cup olive oil
¼ cup lime juice
1 clove garlic, minced
2 teaspoons ground cumin
1 teaspoon chili powder
3 pounds boneless, skinless chicken breast halves (chicken tenders also work)
Salt and pepper, to taste (if desired)
3 green chilies
1 red pepper, seeded and cut into ¾-inch-wide strips
2 red onions, sliced into ½-inch rounds and separated into rings
12 8-inch flour tortillas
Optional toppings: Salsa, grated cheese, sliced or diced avocados, sliced black olives

Preheat grill to medium-high heat. Create a marinade by pureeing cilantro, olive oil, lime juice, garlic, cumin, and chili powder in a blender or food processor. Place chicken in a glass baking dish and pour ⅓ of this marinade over chicken, turning to coat all sides. Season with salt and pepper, if desired. Transfer chicken to the barbecue. Grill chicken until cooked through (7–10 minutes per side, depending on thickness of chicken).

While chicken is cooking, slice chilies, red pepper, and onions; arrange on a rimmed grilling or baking pan. Pour ⅓ of marinade over vegetables. Season with salt and pepper, if desired.

Remove cooked chicken from grill and transfer to a work surface. Grill vegetables until tender, approximately 15 minutes, turning often. Meanwhile, slice chicken crosswise into strips.

Grill tortillas until charred, about 1 minute per side. Fill tortillas with chicken and vegetables and drizzle with remaining marinade. Serve with your favorite salsa and toppings.

Ham and Asparagus Panini

Yield: 2 servings | **Prep Time:** 15 minutes

The panini may have originated in Italy, but its popularity has spread around the world. In the USA, UK, and Canada, this pressed and toasted sandwich ("toastie" to many) is usually made on a panini press to give it those trademark grooves. If you don't own a press, don't despair—you can still enjoy your own version of this sandwich by simply toasting it in a frying pan and placing a foil-covered brick on top of the sandwich.

6 stalks thin asparagus, washed well and trimmed
2 tablespoons mayonnaise
2 teaspoons Dijon mustard
Olive oil
Salt and pepper, to taste
2 slices panini bread (ciabatta or focaccia also work well)
4 slices Muenster cheese
8 ounces sliced deli ham (Black Forest, honey, or smoked work well)

Steam asparagus for about 2 minutes. Cool. In a small bowl, mix mayonnaise and mustard; set aside. Drizzle olive oil on asparagus and season with salt and pepper to taste. Place asparagus on a panini press for 1–2 minutes; remove. Place 1 slice of bread on the panini press; top with 1 slice cheese, 4 ounces of ham, 3 stalks asparagus, and another slice of cheese. Spread mayonnaise-mustard mixture on another piece of bread and place on sandwich. Press or grill sandwich until bread is golden brown and cheese is melted.

Mango and Fish Tacos

Yield: 4 servings | **Prep Time:** 30 minutes | **Cook Time:** 4–6 minutes

The delightful and unusual flavor of mango pairs with the distinct and savory flavor of spiced fish to create a taco not to be missed. This filling is also terrific atop a bed of fresh greens as a salad!

1 pound white fish fillets (cod, halibut, or tilapia)
Olive oil
1–2 tablespoons Cajun spice
Salt and pepper, to taste
1 dozen corn tortillas, warmed*
Mango salsa
Red onion, chopped
Avocado
Lettuce, shredded
Cheddar cheese, grated

Rinse the fish in cold water and pat dry with paper towels. Heat a large skillet to medium-high heat. Add olive oil. When oil is hot, place fish in skillet. Sprinkle with Cajun spice and salt and pepper to taste. If the fillets are thin, they may only need 1 minute of cooking per side; judge cooking time according to thickness of the fillets. When done, fish should be barely transparent and flakey (be careful not to overcook and dry out the fish). Remove fish from heat and place on a plate. Serve in warmed tortillas with mango salsa, red onion, avocado, lettuce, and cheese.

*To warm tortillas, place on a paper towel and heat in a microwave for 20 seconds on high. You can also lightly butter each tortilla and heat both sides briefly in a hot cast-iron skillet.

Saucy Beef Sliders

Yield: Approximately 1 cup sauce; 4 sliders | **Prep Time:** 10 minutes

This is a yummy and fun way to enjoy a sandwich! The sauce for these is delicious and versatile. In fact, it's the sauce that makes this slider special. Try it on BLTs as well.

SAUCE
½ cup mayonnaise
½ cup sour cream
¼ cup chili sauce

4 small ciabatta or other crusty dinner rolls
4 slices roast beef
4 thick slices tomato

Mix sauce ingredients until well blended; refrigerate. When ready to serve, toast both sides of each roll. Spread with sauce and top with roast beef and tomato slices.

Salad Bar Chicken Pitas

A wonderful pita sandwich that travels well to work—also perfect for a picnic. The teriyaki sauce gives this a special zip that will keep your family coming back for more!

TERIYAKI SAUCE:
Yield: 2 cups filling | **Prep Time:** 10 minutes

1¼ cups water, divided
¼ cup tamari soy sauce
¼ cup brown sugar
2 cloves garlic, minced
1 tablespoon fresh grated ginger
2 tablespoons cornstarch

In a medium saucepan, combine 1 cup water, soy sauce, brown sugar, garlic, and ginger; bring to a boil, stirring constantly. Dissolve cornstarch in remaining ¼ cup water and add to sauce. Stir constantly to allow sauce to thicken. If the sauce is too thick, add a little more water or soy sauce to thin it.

CHICKEN PITA FILLING
Yield: Filling for 8 pita halves | **Prep Time:** 20 minutes

1 pound boneless, skinless chicken breasts, cut in strips
¼ cup teriyaki sauce (from recipe above)
1 teaspoon minced garlic
4 whole pita bread rounds, cut in half

8 chopped lettuce leaves
2 medium tomatoes, thinly sliced
Alfalfa sprouts

In a small bowl, combine chicken strips, teriyaki sauce, and garlic. Coat a large nonstick skillet with cooking spray. Heat over medium-high heat until hot. Add chicken mixture and cook 8–10 minutes or until chicken is no longer pink inside. Remove from heat and keep warm. Fill each pita half with chicken, lettuce, tomato, and alfalfa sprouts. If desired, add additional teriyaki sauce.

Tuscan White Bean and Tuna Sandwich

Yield: 4 servings | **Prep Time:** 10 minutes

Tuna, a heart-healthy fish, teams up with blood sugar-lowering white beans. High in protein and low in fat, there couldn't be a better combination when trying to eat a healthy diet.

1½ tablespoons olive oil
1 tablespoon red wine vinegar
1 15-ounce can small white beans, rinsed and drained
1 6-ounce can solid white albacore tuna, packed in water
⅓ cup finely chopped red onion
½ cup water chestnuts, drained and diced
¼ teaspoon salt
¼ teaspoon pepper
4 ciabatta rolls, split and toasted
Mayonnaise, for spreading on rolls
2 cups packed fresh baby spinach
1 medium tomato, sliced
1 small red onion, sliced

In a small bowl, whisk olive oil and vinegar. In a medium bowl, coarsely mash beans and tuna; add onion, water chestnuts, salt, pepper, and half the vinegar mixture. Brush rolls with remaining vinegar mixture and spread with mayonnaise. Divide the spinach among the bottom roll halves. Place tomato slice and red onion slice atop spinach; top with tuna mixture and remaining roll halves.

Steak Sandwich Supreme

Yield: 4 sandwiches | **Prep Time:** 10 minutes | **Cook Time:** 6 minutes

Sandwiches have evolved to include wraps, pitas, submarines, hoagies, paninis, and sliders. No matter the format, one thing is for sure: Sandwiches are here to stay. And this quick, easy Steak Sandwich Supreme may be the granddaddy of them all.

4 rolls, split in half
Butter
3 tablespoons oil
1½ pounds top sirloin steak, thinly sliced
½ teaspoon Worcestershire sauce
1 medium sweet onion, sliced
1 medium bell pepper, cut into strips
4 ounces fresh mushrooms, sliced
¼ teaspoon salt
¼ teaspoon pepper
1 teaspoon Italian seasoning
Garlic Parmesan spread (recipe follows)
8 slices Swiss cheese
1 large tomato, cut into 8 thin slices

Preheat oven to 475° F. Butter rolls; toast in oven until lightly browned. Set aside.

Heat olive oil in a large skillet over medium-high heat. Cook steak for 2 minutes, then sprinkle with Worcestershire sauce. Add onions and bell peppers and cook for another 2 minutes. Add mushrooms and cook for 1–2 minutes. Add salt, pepper, and Italian seasoning.

Cover toasted buns with Garlic Parmesan Spread (recipe follows); leftover spread may be covered and refrigerated for later use. Place the steak and vegetable mixture on the toasted buns and top each sandwich with Swiss cheese and tomato. Finish with more spread.

GARLIC PARMESAN SPREAD

½ cup mayonnaise
2 cloves garlic, minced
1 tablespoon finely grated Parmesan cheese

Mix all ingredients until thoroughly blended.

Chicken Salad Croissant

Yield: 6–8 servings | **Prep Time:** 25 minutes

This sandwich packs well, so it is perfect for a brown-bag lunch. It's also wonderful as a light dinner. This recipe is easily halved or doubled.

1½ cups water
1 pound boneless, skinless chicken breasts
1 cup mayonnaise
2 teaspoons fresh lemon juice
8 fresh basil leaves, minced
Salt and pepper, to taste
2 cups seedless grapes, halved
¾–1 cup roughly chopped cashews (or sliced almonds)
2 ribs celery, diced
6–7 green onions, diced
½ cup peeled and diced jicama
6–8 plain croissants, split in half
Lettuce leaves
6–8 Havarti cheese slices

To quickly cook chicken, bring 1½ cups water to a boil in a large skillet. Add chicken, cover, and reduce heat; simmer for 10–15 minutes, or until chicken is cooked through. Drain, chop into bite-size pieces, and let cool.

In a large bowl, mix mayonnaise, lemon juice, basil, and salt and pepper until well combined. Fold in grapes, nuts, celery, onions, jicama, and cooked chicken. Fill croissants with salad, lettuce, and cheese slices.

Main Dishes

Resisting the allure of the drive-through window will be easy with these delicious recipes, which range from the proverbial pot roast to a traditional calzone. If you need a little help breaking out of a mealtime rut, look no further. Here are unique, scrumptious, and, yes, lovely-to-look-at dishes that will satisfy the creative cook in you and the desire for a great meal in your family and friends!

Slow-Cooked Artichoke Chicken
Yield: 6–8 servings | **Prep Time:** 20 minute | **Cook Time:** 5–6 hours

High in fiber and antioxidants, artichokes are a welcome addition to this divine chicken dish. Serve this easy recipe over cooked rice for a hearty meal fit for the hungriest crowd.

3 boneless, skinless chicken breasts
1 teaspoon salt
1 teaspoon paprika
1 teaspoon cayenne pepper
2 tablespoons olive oil
3 tablespoons white balsamic vinegar
2 cloves garlic, minced
2 leeks, washed well and thinly sliced (discard the tough, dark green leaves)
8 ounces frozen artichoke hearts
1½ cups chicken broth

Season chicken pieces with salt, paprika, and cayenne pepper. In a large skillet over medium-high heat, brown chicken on all sides in olive oil. Remove chicken from skillet and place in slow-cooker. Add balsamic vinegar, garlic, and leeks to skillet and stir for 1 minute; stir in artichoke hearts and chicken broth. Pour skillet ingredients over chicken in slow-cooker. Cover and cook on LOW for 5–6 hours.

Marinated Brisket

Yield: 8 servings | **Marinating Time:** 12 hours | **Bake Time:** 6–8 hours

This recipe, which always receives rave reviews, has been the centerpiece many times at neighborhood gatherings, family celebrations, and church potlucks. Now it's your turn to try the best brisket ever!

1 3-pound brisket
1–2 tablespoons onion salt
1–2 tablespoons garlic salt
1–2 tablespoons celery salt
1 16-ounce bottle barbeque sauce
½ of a 5-ounce bottle liquid smoke
½ cup plus 3 tablespoons Worcestershire sauce

Sprinkle brisket with onion salt, garlic salt, and celery salt to taste. Place in heavy foil. Pour full bottle of barbecue sauce over meat. Wrap the foil around the meat and refrigerate for 12 hours. Remove from refrigerator, open foil, and add liquid smoke and Worcestershire sauce. Re-seal foil and bake in marinade at 275° F for 6–8 hours. Baking the brisket on low heat for several hours is the secret to its delicious flavor.

Lemon-Basil Grilled Chicken

Yield: 8 servings | **Prep Time:** 15 minutes | **Marinating Time:** Overnight
Grill Time: 15 minutes

This is an exceptional alternative to the traditional barbecue sauce typically used on chicken. Marinating your chicken overnight ensures that you end up with moist, tender chicken every time!

1 cup extra-virgin olive oil
1 cup lemon juice
4 teaspoons minced onion
2 teaspoons salt
2 tablespoons chopped basil (or more, to taste)
4 cloves garlic
8 boneless, skinless chicken breast halves

In a blender or food processor, blend the oil, lemon juice, onion, salt, basil, and garlic until thick and smooth. Reserve half the marinade to use as a basting sauce for grilling; refrigerate reserved marinade. Pour remaining marinade into a flat container. Coat chicken pieces in marinade; cover container. Refrigerate overnight.

When ready to grill, cover the grill grate with aluminum foil and poke holes in the foil. Preheat the grill for high heat. Spray foil with cooking spray and lay chicken on foiled grate. Baste with reserved basil marinade. Cook 7½ minutes, brushing frequently with marinade. Turn chicken pieces. Cook 7½ more minutes or until juices run clear, brushing often with marinade.

TIP: To facilitate even grilling, pound chicken until each breast is the same thickness.

Asparagus Chicken Cordon Bleu

Yield: 2 servings | **Prep Time:** 15 minutes | **Bake Time:** 20–25 minutes

This is the perfect main course for a special-occasion dinner. Easy to prepare, delicious, and pretty, this dish is one we often turn to when we want something extraordinary. It's easy to double, and why not? The leftovers are just as amazing the second time around!

2 boneless, skinless chicken breasts
1 tablespoon Dijon mustard
¼ teaspoon onion salt
10 asparagus spears, trimmed
2 slices thin deli ham
2 slices Havarti cheese
Fresh ground pepper, to taste
3 tablespoons butter-flavored crackers, crushed (Keebler Club Crackers®, Ritz®, etc.)
Almond slivers, for garnish (optional)

Preheat oven to 350° F. Pound chicken to about ¼ inch thickness. Spread with mustard and sprinkle with onion salt. Place asparagus spears (5 per breast) down the center of the chicken. Place ham and cheese slices atop asparagus; fold chicken over and secure with toothpicks if necessary.

   Place seam side down in an ungreased 8-inch square baking dish. Pepper chicken to taste. Sprinkle with cracker crumbs. Bake uncovered for 20–25 minutes, or until chicken juices run clear. This can be served with your favorite Hollandaise sauce, but it's so juicy and flavorful that there's no real need for a sauce. We like to garnish with almond slivers when we have them.

Butter and Honey Pork Loin

Yield: 2 servings | **Prep Time:** 20 minutes | **Bake Time:** 20–25 minutes

This elegant dish with easy ingredients is so simple to prepare. Serve this with oven-roasted potatoes and vegetables—they can be roasting while the loin is baking!

4½ tablespoons butter
2 tablespoons honey
1½ pounds pork tenderloin, trimmed of silver skin
½ teaspoon salt
½ teaspoon pepper
¼ cup apple juice

Preheat oven to 375° F. In a Dutch oven or ovenproof skillet, heat butter and honey over medium heat, stirring to melt butter.

Season the pork with salt and pepper and place in prepared skillet. Cook until underside is lightly browned, approximately 5 minutes. Turn pork and cook until other side is browned, approximately 5 more minutes. Lower the heat if the honey mixture starts to burn. Place pan in oven and roast until the loin is just cooked through, approximately 20–25 minutes or until a meat thermometer inserted into the thickest part of the cut reads 145° F.

Transfer pork to a warm plate and cover with foil to rest for 3 minutes. Meanwhile, add apple juice to pan, stirring over medium heat to scrape up all the browned bits (we call them "the goodness"). Add any accumulated pork juices from the resting plate, and simmer until sauce is reduced to about ½ cup. Slice loin on the diagonal and drizzle with sauce prior to serving. Store any leftover meat in the refrigerator, tightly wrapped, to keep it moist.

Picnic Fried Chicken

Yield: 4 servings | **Prep Time:** 30 minutes
Marinating Time: 1 hour to overnight | **Cook Time:** 40 minutes

For many families, a picnic just isn't a picnic without fried chicken. This recipe has been tested on the most demanding of chicken connoisseurs, and the applause is deafening!

3 pounds chicken legs, thighs, or breasts
1 quart buttermilk

CHICKEN COATING

4 cups flour
4 teaspoons sea salt
1 teaspoon black pepper
1 teaspoon garlic powder
1 teaspoon onion powder
2 tablespoons paprika
½ teaspoon ground sage
½ teaspoon ground thyme
¼ teaspoon baking powder
Canola oil for frying (approximately 1
    quart)

Wash chicken pieces and dry with paper towels; place in a large, shallow dish. Pour buttermilk over chicken; cover and allow to soak at least 1 hour or overnight in the refrigerator.

When ready to fry the chicken, prepare coating. Combine all ingredients in a large zip-top plastic bag. Add chicken pieces, one at a time, and shake to coat chicken well. Allow coated pieces to rest on waxed paper at least 15 minutes (the coating will dry and cling better during frying). After 15 minutes, once again shake the chicken pieces in the coating mixture. This double application is the secret to the coating clinging to the chicken during frying.

In an electric skillet, heat 1½ inches oil to 350°–360° F; fry chicken, turning occasionally, for a total of 20–25 minutes or until juices run clear and chicken is tender.

Grilled Veggie Pizza

Yield: 4 servings | **Prep Time:** 10 minutes | **Grill Time:** 10 minutes

Kaycee and her family love this recipe and use it all the time as a fun and healthy change from the typical campout hot dog roast. Just pop your pizza onto an oiled veggie roaster or use tinfoil with holes poked into it to cover your grill grate.

⅓ cup mayonnaise
3 cloves garlic, minced
1 tablespoon lemon juice
2 tablespoons extra-virgin olive oil
1 cup thinly sliced red bell peppers
1 small zucchini, thinly sliced
1 red onion, thinly sliced
1 small yellow squash, thinly sliced
4 small Boboli® thin pizza crusts
1 cup crumbled feta cheese (can use other
    types of cheese)

In a small bowl, mix mayonnaise, garlic, and lemon juice. Set aside in the refrigerator.

Oil a vegetable roaster or cover your grill with oiled foil and poke holes in the foil. Preheat grill for high heat. Brush vegetables with olive oil on each side.

Arrange veggies on foil or vegetable roaster: place bell pepper and zucchini closest to the middle of the grill, and set onion and yellow squash pieces around them. Cook for about 3 minutes, turn, and cook for another 3 minutes. Remove vegetables from grill (the peppers may need to stay on and cook a few minutes longer) and set aside.

Grill pizza crusts for 1 minute on both sides to set crust. Spread each pizza crust with mayonnaise mixture and sprinkle each one with feta cheese. Place on the grill, cheese side up. Close grill lid (or cover pizza with a foil tent) and cook for 2–3 minutes. This will warm the pizza crusts and slightly melt the cheese. Watch carefully so the bottoms don't burn. Remove from grill and layer crusts with grilled vegetables. Serve immediately.

Fiesta Stuffed Shells

Yield: 38 large pasta shells | **Prep Time:** 20 minutes | **Bake Time:** 30 minutes

This unusual, enticing, and versatile dish can be made with ground beef or leftover turkey, as well as chicken. It can be made up to 2 days prior to serving or can be made and frozen for up to 2 months. Who doesn't need a main dish recipe like this in their mealtime arsenal?

38 large pasta shells
4 boneless, skinless chicken breasts, cooked and finely chopped
1 15-ounce can black beans
1 medium red onion, finely chopped
2 whole sweet bell peppers (any color), finely chopped
1–2 teaspoons ground cumin
1 8-ounce package cream cheese, softened
1 14.5-ounce can diced tomatoes, undrained
1 4-ounce can diced green chilies
¼ cup chicken stock
1 cup picanté sauce, divided
½ cup cheddar cheese, finely shredded

Cook pasta shells *al dente* (firm) according to package directions, about 8 minutes. The shells will be easier to stuff when firm (they'll continue cooking in the oven). Chicken can be grilled, boiled, baked, or even canned.

Preheat oven to 350° F. In a large bowl, mix chicken, black beans, onion, peppers, and cumin. In a separate large bowl, mix cream cheese, tomatoes, chilies, and chicken stock. Blend mixture until all ingredients are incorporated. Pour over chicken mixture. Spoon combined mixture into shells.

Spread ½ cup picanté sauce in the bottom of a 13 x 18 x 2-inch pan or use two 9 x 13-inch pans. Arrange shells in pan and drizzle with remaining picanté sauce; sprinkle with cheese. Cover pan with foil and bake for 30 minutes until hot and bubbly. Add extra picanté sauce if desired.

TIP: All ingredients can be prepared ahead and stored in small containers in the refrigerator to await later assembly and baking, if desired.

Old-Fashioned Chicken Pot Pie

Yield: 6–8 servings | **Prep Time:** 30 minutes | **Bake Time:** 50 minutes

Family and friends will love having pot pie made from scratch! Wholesome vegetables and succulent chicken are combined into a savory white sauce that binds the dish together. One serving is never enough, so be sure to make one or two extra of these delicious pies.

1 pound boneless, skinless chicken breast
    halves, cubed
1 cup sliced carrots
1 cup frozen peas
½ cup sliced celery
¼ cup butter
½ cup chopped onion
⅓ cup flour
½ teaspoon salt
¼ teaspoon pepper
¼ teaspoon celery seed
2–3 cloves garlic, minced
1¾ cups chicken broth
⅔ cup milk
2 9-inch unbaked piecrusts (try Jeanne's
    No-Fail Pie Crust, page 203)

Preheat oven to 350° F. In a saucepan, combine chicken, carrots, peas, and celery. Cover with water and boil for 15 minutes. Remove from heat; drain, remove to a bowl, and set aside.

In the same saucepan, melt butter and cook onions over medium heat until soft and translucent. Stir in flour, salt, pepper, celery seed, and garlic. Slowly stir in chicken broth and milk. Simmer over medium-low heat until thick. Add chicken and vegetables to sauce. Remove from heat and set aside.

Line pie pan with crust. Pour hot chicken mixture into crust and top with second crust. Cut away excess dough and seal edges. Make several small slits in the top to allow steam to escape.

Bake for 50 minutes, or until pastry is golden brown and filling is bubbly. Cool for 10 minutes before serving.

TIP: This recipe adapts well to small, single-serve baking dishes.

Fresh Pesto Lasagna

Yield: 10 servings | **Prep Time:** 35 minutes | **Bake Time:** 50 minutes

Not a typical lasagna, this delicious pasta dish pairs well with a tossed salad and crusty French bread for a superb Sunday evening dinner.

16 lasagna noodles
1⅓ cups grated Parmesan cheese, divided
Béchamel sauce (recipe follows)
Pesto (recipe follows)

Preheat oven to 375° F. Cook pasta according to package directions; drain well. Lay noodles in a single layer onto buttered waxed paper to prevent them from sticking together.

Spread 1 cup Béchamel sauce over bottom of a buttered 9 x 13-inch baking dish. Place 4 noodles atop sauce. Spread 1 cup Béchamel sauce over noodles. Spoon 1⅓ cups pesto sauce over the Béchamel sauce. Sprinkle ⅓ cup Parmesan cheese over pesto sauce. Repeat layers 2 more times: 4 more noodles, 1 cup Béchamel sauce, 1⅓ cups pesto sauce, and ⅓ cup cheese.

Finish assembly with last 4 noodles, 1 cup Béchamel sauce, and ⅓ cup Parmesan cheese. Cover lasagna with foil and bake for 30 minutes. Uncover and bake 20 more minutes. Let sit 10 minutes before serving.

BÉCHAMEL SAUCE

½ cup butter
⅓ cup minced shallots
½ cup flour
4 cups milk
1 bay leaf
¼ teaspoon ground nutmeg
Salt and pepper, to taste

In a large saucepan over medium heat, melt butter. Stir in shallots; sauté 2 minutes. Add flour and whisk until smooth. Reduce heat to low and whisk 1 minute. Gradually whisk in milk. Bring to a boil, whisking constantly. Add bay leaf. Reduce heat and simmer until slightly thickened, about 5 minutes. Mix in nutmeg. Season with salt and pepper to taste. Remove bay leaf and let cool.

PESTO

2 cups fresh basil leaves, well packed
1 cup grated Parmesan cheese
½ cup extra-virgin olive oil
¼ cup pine nuts
4 small cloves garlic, halved
1 cup vegetable broth
Salt and pepper, to taste

In a food processor, blend basil, Parmesan cheese, olive oil, pine nuts, and garlic until a coarse purée forms. Lightly mix in vegetable broth. Season with salt and pepper to taste. Let cool.

Rave City Ribs

Yield: 6 servings | **Prep Time:** 15 minutes | **Grill Time:** 20 minutes

These delicious ribs are infused with apple juice before being coated with a perfectly balanced blend of spices and being grilled until tender. You'll think twice before going out for ribs, now that you've discovered this recipe. There's a good reason these ribs are called "Rave City"!

2 teaspoons cumin
½ tablespoon smoked paprika
1 tablespoon garlic powder
1 tablespoon onion powder
2 teaspoons chili powder
1 tablespoon brown sugar
2 tablespoons salt
¼ teaspoon cayenne pepper
1 teaspoon celery salt
1 full rack pork or beef ribs (approximately 5 pounds)
2 quarts apple juice
Canola oil

In a large bowl, combine all dry ingredients; mix well. In a large pot, boil ribs in the apple juice for 10 minutes. This pre-cooking not only adds flavor but also helps to remove extra fat. Remove ribs from juice and cool.

Preheat grill to high (approximately 400°–425° F). When ribs have cooled, rub with canola oil, coating thoroughly—this helps the rub adhere to the ribs. Rub the mixture into the ribs well.

Grill on high for 8–10 minutes on each side or until meat is tender. If desired, serve with your favorite barbecue sauce.

Ultimate Sunday Pot Roast

Yield: 6–8 servings | **Prep Time:** 20 minutes | **Cook Time:** 2–2½ hours

Nothing beats the aroma of a roast being cooked! This recipe works well with prime rib also, but whatever cut of beef used, the crispy outer crust of each moist slice is delectable. "Ultimate" is certainly the word for this special roast—a roast our families have savored on many special occasions.

Extra-virgin olive oil, for coating skillet and roasting pan
1 7-pound rump or rib roast
1 6-ounce jar prepared horseradish
1 cup fresh parsley, chopped
¼ cup Grey Poupon Harvest Coarse-Ground Mustard®
1½ teaspoons kosher or sea salt
1 teaspoon coarsely ground pepper

Preheat oven to 375° F. In a well-oiled skillet over high heat, sear all sides of the roast. Remove from heat and let cool. Coat bottom of roasting pan with olive oil; place roast in pan. Pour horseradish into a medium bowl; with paper towels, blot out as much liquid as possible to achieve a "dry" texture. Combine horseradish, parsley, mustard, salt, and pepper; mix well.

Using your hands, rub this mixture over entire roast, making a "crust." Bake for 2–2½ hours, uncovered. Remove roast and let sit for 15 minutes to allow juices to redistribute before slicing.

Feta Lemon Chicken

Yield: 6 servings | **Prep Time:** 15 minutes | **Bake Time:** 10–15 minutes

It doesn't matter how good something is for you if it doesn't taste good! This is one of those recipes that tastes so good you can't believe it's also good for you.

2 pounds boneless, skinless chicken breasts,
    cut into strips
Salt and pepper to taste
¼ cup extra-virgin olive oil, divided
3 lemons, juiced
¼ teaspoon lemon zest
½ teaspoon thyme
½ teaspoon basil
¼ teaspoon onion salt
¾ cup crumbled feta cheese

Preheat oven to 350° F. Salt and pepper chicken strips to taste. Cook strips in 2 tablespoons olive oil approximately 2 minutes on each side or until brown. They will finish cooking in the oven. Lay chicken strips quickly on a paper towel to remove excess oil and then place them in a 9 x 13-inch baking dish. Mix lemon juice, lemon zest, 2 additional tablespoons olive oil, thyme, basil, and onion salt until well blended. Pour mixture over chicken strips.

Sprinkle with feta cheese; bake for 10–15 minutes.

TIP ON COOKING CHICKEN SO IT STAYS MOIST: Chicken is easy to overbake, and you can't afford to be careless with oven temperatures or bake times. No matter what chicken recipe you're using, you will get a juicier baked chicken if you brine your chicken overnight in salt water (1 cup salt to 4 cups water). Coat your chicken pieces either in mayonnaise, buttermilk, undiluted cream of chicken soup, or dry Italian dressing mix before rolling them in your breading mixture.

Many-Way Meatballs

Yield: 24 meatballs | **Prep Time:** 20 minutes | **Baking Time:** 25–30 minutes

Meat sauce can stand alone, but including meatballs is always a welcome addition and an easy way to "beef up" (pun intended) a main dish. These are the perfect meal-in-a-flash weapon to keep in the freezer—simply by changing their size, adjusting the ingredients a bit, or varying the sauce in which they sit, you end up with all sorts of wonderful entrees!

1 pound ground beef
1 pound ground sausage
2 eggs
½ cup milk
2 cups bread crumbs
½ cup chopped onion
½ cup grated Parmesan cheese
2 tablespoons tomato paste
1 tablespoon chopped fresh parsley
1 teaspoon crushed oregano
¾ teaspoon black pepper
½ teaspoon garlic powder
1 teaspoon salt

In a large bowl, mix ground meats using an electric mixer. In a separate medium bowl, mix eggs, milk, bread crumbs, onion, cheese, tomato paste, parsley, and all seasonings. Add egg mixture to meat mixture and combine thoroughly. Spray two large baking sheets with cooking spray. Form meatballs; place a small distance apart on baking sheets. Cover with plastic wrap and freeze for approximately 3 hours. Remove frozen balls from pans and place in labeled zip-top plastic bags or freezer containers.

To cook: In the refrigerator, thaw the amount you need for your recipe. Add the thawed meatballs to your recipe—such as spaghetti sauce and stroganoff (recipes follow)—and simmer for about 30 minutes. Alternately, bake the meatballs on a lightly oiled sheet at 350° F for 25 minutes or fry them over medium-low heat until crispy and cooked through.

MEATBALL MUSHROOM STROGANOFF
3 tablespoons extra-virgin olive oil
½ cup chopped onion
1 clove garlic, minced
1 cup mushrooms, sliced

1 cup beef or chicken stock
2 tablespoons cornstarch
2 cups half-and-half or whole milk
24 meatballs, precooked
2 tablespoons chopped fresh dill or parsley
½ cup sour cream
Salt and pepper, to taste
4 cups rice, cooked

In a large pan, heat oil; add onion and garlic. Cook over medium heat until onion and garlic are softened, about 5 minutes. Add the mushrooms and cook 5 more minutes. Stir in the beef or chicken stock and bring to a boil, stirring frequently.

In a small bowl, mix cornstarch with half-and-half until smooth. Add to pan and stir until thickened. Add the precooked meatballs, dill, sour cream, salt, and pepper. Reduce heat to low and cook until the meatballs are heated through. Serve over hot rice.

MINUTE SPAGHETTI MARINARA

1 29-ounce can tomato sauce
3 garlic cloves, minced
1 medium onion, chopped
1 teaspoon dried basil
2 tablespoons butter
Salt and freshly ground pepper to taste

In a medium saucepan, combine all ingredients. Bring to a simmer and lower heat to maintain a simmer; cook for 15–20 minutes, stirring occasionally.

TIP: For a smooth sauce, process or blend before serving.

MORE MEATBALL MEAL IDEAS:

1. Swedish meatballs served with red potatoes
2. Sweet and sour meatballs over rice
3. Party appetizer balls
4. Barbecue meatball subs with bleu cheese
5. Meatball minestrone soup

Citrus Grilled Salmon on Greens

Yield: 4 servings | **Prep Time:** 10 minutes | **Marinating Time:** 1–2 hours
Grill Time: Approximately 8 minutes

Whether you're a novice or a pro, this recipe will make you look like a genius. Thanks to the marinade, there's very little chance these fillets will end up dry and uninteresting. And this stunning combination of flavors will convert even the toughest fish skeptics.

Extra-virgin olive oil
4 6-ounce, 1-inch-thick salmon fillets
Kosher salt, to taste
Freshly cracked black pepper, to taste

MARINADE
¾ cup fresh orange juice
¼ cup fresh lemon juice
¼ cup fresh lime juice
1 clove garlic, minced
2 tablespoons orange marmalade
2 tablespoons soy sauce
1 tablespoon light brown sugar
2 tablespoons minced cilantro
1 tablespoon butter
Pinch kosher salt
Freshly cracked black pepper, to taste
4–5 cups fresh salad greens

In a medium saucepan, combine all marinade ingredients and bring to a boil over medium heat, stirring constantly to melt the marmalade and to keep the mixture from burning. Reduce heat to a simmer and let the marinade reduce until syrupy, about 15–20 minutes. Add additional salt and pepper to taste. Pour marinade into a large, shallow container; set salmon fillets in marinade and cover. Refrigerate for 1–2 hours.

When ready to cook, heat grill to medium-high heat. Brush both sides of salmon fillets with olive oil just before grilling; season with salt and pepper to taste. Grill salmon for approximately 4 minutes per side, brushing with marinade during the final few minutes of cooking. Transfer salmon to bed of greens and garnish with extra cilantro leaves if desired.

Dinner in a Squash

Yield: 6 servings | **Prep Time:** 30 minutes | **Bake Time:** 1 hour

This is a fun twist on a typical dinner in a pumpkin. Acorn squash is a good choice because, depending on the size of the squash, everyone can have his or her own. If you use large squash, the halves can be cut in half again, as this is a hearty, full meal.

3 large acorn squash
1 pound ground beef
½ cup celery, chopped
1 small green pepper, chopped
1 small onion, chopped
½ cup soy sauce
2 tablespoons brown sugar
1 4-ounce can sliced mushrooms, drained
1 10¾-ounce can condensed cream of chicken soup
2 cups cooked rice

Preheat oven to 375° F. Wash each squash well; lay each on side and cut in half. Remove all fibers and seeds. Set aside. In a large skillet, cook beef, celery, green pepper, and onion until meat is browned and vegetables are tender; drain. Add all remaining ingredients and cook an additional 3 minutes, mixing well. Divide filling among the 6 squash halves and place them on a large parchment-lined baking sheet. Bake for 1 hour.

Traditional Calzone

Yield: 10 calzones | **Bake Time:** Approximately 15–18 minutes

Italian food is a popular choice for dinner (and lunch; shoot, we even have leftovers for break-fast!), and traditional calzones are at the top of the list. Won't your crowd be pleased and excited when you set a platter of these at your table?

CALZONES PIZZA DOUGH

Yield: 10 3-inch balls | **Prep Time:** Approximately 50 minutes

5 cups flour
1½ teaspoons salt
4½ teaspoons sugar
2 tablespoons rapid-rise yeast
2 tablespoons extra-virgin olive oil
2 cups hot water
2 tablespoons dried basil
2 tablespoons dried Parmesan or Romano cheese
Egg whites, for basting calzones

In a mixer bowl, combine flour, salt, sugar, and yeast; blend well. Add oil and water; blend until a soft dough forms. Knead for 10 minutes. Place dough in large buttered bowl; cover with a damp cloth and let rise in warmed oven for approximately 30 minutes.

Preheat oven to 350° F. Punch down dough and divide into 10 balls. Allow dough to "rest." Working with one ball at a time, form into an approximate 6-inch circle. Place ⅓ cup calzone filling (recipe follows) on each circle. Fold circle in half; seal edges. Blend dried basil and Parmesan cheese. Baste each calzone with egg white and sprinkle basil-cheese mixture over calzones.

Place calzones on parchment-lined baking sheet. Bake for 15–18 minutes or until golden brown. Serve hot with favorite marinara sauce. Refrigerate leftovers—they are good cold and make an excellent brown-bag lunch or picnic take-along.

CALZONE FILLING
Yield: Approximately 8 cups |
Prep Time: 30 minutes (does not include making dough)

1 pound mild Italian sausage, cooked and drained
1 pound ground beef, cooked and drained
1 6-ounce can tomato paste
1 8-ounce can tomato sauce
½ cup finely diced green or red pepper
½ cup finely diced onion
½ cup chopped black olives
2 cloves garlic, minced
1 tablespoon Italian seasoning
1 cup grated Parmesan cheese
3 cups grated mozzarella cheese, divided

In a large bowl, mix all ingredients, reserving 1 cup mozzarella. Stir well so all ingredients are coated with tomato sauce. Just before sealing each calzone, sprinkle a little of the reserved mozzarella over filling, then finish by tightly sealing dough.

Salmon with Fresh Fruit Salsa

Yield: 4 servings fish, approximately 4 cups salsa | **Prep Time:** 15 minutes | **Bake Time:** 12 minutes

Salmon is a heart-healthy favorite that takes on different personalities, depending on what it's paired with. This special salsa takes salmon, and any other fish, to a whole new level!

Extra-virgin olive oil, to coat baking pan and fish
4 6-ounce, 1-inch-thick salmon fillets
1 cup water
¼ cup lemon juice
Kosher salt, to taste
Freshly cracked black pepper, to taste

Preheat oven to 350° F. Coat baking pan and fillets with olive oil. Mix water and lemon juice; pour over fish. Sprinkle salt and pepper over fish. Cover pan and bake at 350° F for approximately 12 minutes or until fish flakes.

SALSA

1 cup fresh pineapple, diced
¾ cup fresh mango, diced
1½ cups fresh strawberries, hulled and diced
¼ cup finely chopped red onion
1 scant teaspoon ginger (fresh or even less if using ground)
2½ tablespoons fresh lemon juice
2 teaspoons sugar
2 teaspoons finely chopped cilantro

In a large mixing bowl, fold all ingredients. Remove 1 cup; using a blender, blend until smooth. Return blended mixture to ingredients in bowl and mix together until all ingredients are coated well. Serve ⅓ to ½ cup salsa over fish; place extra salsa in serving container and serve with fish.

TIP: This delicious salsa can also be substituted for calorie- and fat-laden salad dressings. Just pour ½ cup or more over your bed of greens and enjoy!

Lasagna Cupcakes

Yield: 6 large cupcakes | **Prep Time:** 30 minutes | **Bake Time:** 25–30 minutes + 10 minutes standing

Lasagna made into cupcakes! Who knew? Prepare to dazzle and delight family and friends with this scrumptious and fun-to-eat twist on a time-tested favorite.

SAUCE

½ pound ground beef or Italian sausage, cooked and drained
3 tablespoons extra-virgin olive oil
½ large onion, chopped
½ medium red bell pepper, chopped
1 small zucchini, diced
3–4 cloves garlic, minced
1 6-ounce can tomato paste
1 8-ounce can tomato sauce
1 14.5-ounce can diced tomatoes
2 tablespoons chopped fresh basil or 1 tablespoon dried basil
¾ tablespoon dried oregano
½ teaspoon salt
¼ teaspoon pepper

CHEESE

1 10-ounce tub Italian herb and cheese cooking cream (found next to cream cheese in the dairy case); other cheeses may be substituted if this isn't available
½ cup grated Parmesan cheese
½ cup ricotta cheese

¾ pound grated mozzarella cheese, divided
½ teaspoon pepper
2 eggs

21 lasagna noodles (approximately 1 16-ounce box)

To prepare sauce: In large pan, cook meat until well browned; drain and remove from pan to a separate bowl. In same pan, heat olive oil over medium heat and sauté onions, red bell pepper, zucchini, and garlic (approximately 5 minutes or until vegetables are soft). Stir in the cooked meat and tomato paste; mix well. Stir in tomato sauce, diced tomatoes, basil, oregano, salt, and pepper; blend well.

For cheese filling: In large bowl, stir together herb and cheese cooking cream (or substitute), Parmesan cheese, ricotta cheese, and half of the mozzarella cheese; add pepper and eggs and mix well.

For noodles: Cook noodles according to package directions, but lessen cooking time by 5 minutes. Drain. Lay noodles on buttered aluminum foil, separated to prevent sticking together.

To assemble: Preheat oven to 350° F and spray a jumbo muffin tin with cooking spray. Line the sides of each muffin cup with 1 noodle; noodle ends will overlap. Cut remaining noodles in fourths. Place one piece on the bottom of each muffin cup. Place ⅛ cup of sauce on bottom of each muffin cup (atop cut noodle). Place ⅛ cup of cheese filling on top of sauce in each cup. Top sauce with another noodle piece, and continue layering, adding sauce and cheese filling until all cups are filled. Finish by topping each cup with the remaining mozzarella cheese. Bake for 25–30 minutes, until cupcakes are browned and bubbly. Remove from oven; let cupcakes rest for approximately 10 minutes. To remove for serving, run a sharp knife around cup edges and carefully lift contents of each cup out, using a large serving spoon.

Bacon Feta Burgers

Yield: 3–4 servings | **Cook Time:** 40–45 minutes

Who doesn't love a good burger? This recipe is one of the best hamburgers we've ever tried—created by a man (Kaycee's husband, Taylor) to cater especially to men. However, we know you women will love them too!

1 pound lean ground beef
¼ cup evaporated milk
½ cup cooked, crumbled bacon
½ teaspoon pepper
1 cup (or more—this is definitely to taste) feta cheese

In a medium bowl, mix ground beef, milk, bacon, and pepper well. Add feta cheese. The best size for these burgers is ¼ to ⅓ pound of meat mixture per burger; the cheese should give the patties a marbled look. Grill to preferred doneness over medium heat.

TIP: You can also use bleu cheese crumbles instead of feta cheese.

Orange Pork Kabobs

Yield: 4 kabob skewers | **Prep Time:** 15 minutes | **Marinating Time:** 2 hours
Grill Time: 10–14 minutes

Kabobs are a griller's favorite—a fun way to combine an exciting spectrum of flavors, textures, and colors. These pretty kabobs have a gourmet look and taste but are so easy to make!

1 pound pork tenderloin
¾ cup apricot preserves
⅓ cup chopped red onion
⅓ cup tamari soy sauce (may substitute regular soy sauce)
1 tablespoon fresh ginger, peeled and minced
2 teaspoons hot chili oil
4 medium yellow onions, halved
1 green pepper, cut into 8 parts
8 1-inch cubes fresh pineapple
1 medium orange, cut into 8 wedges

4 12-inch skewers

Trim fat from pork; cut into 16 1-inch cubes. Combine pork, preserves, chopped onion, tamari sauce, ginger, and chili oil in large zip-top plastic bag. Seal and marinate in refrigerator for 2 hours. Preheat grill to medium-high heat. Remove pork from bag; reserve marinade. Alternating items, thread pork cubes, onion halves, bell pepper pieces, pineapple cubes, and orange wedges onto 4 skewers. Place kabobs on grill. Grill 5–7 minutes on each side until pork is cooked thoroughly, basting with reserved marinade.

NOTE: Do not marinate overnight; the flavors are too strong and will overpower the pork.

Succulent Prime Rib

Yield: Depends on roast size | **Prep Time:** 15 minutes | **Bake Time:** 15–20 minutes/pound + resting time

Is there a more elegant entrée than prime rib? Cooked to perfection, it leaves lasting memories of the meal with all dinner guests.

4– to 6–pound prime rib roast
4–6 tablespoons beef bouillon granules
2 tablespoons garlic granules
1 tablespoon seasoning salt
4 oregano leaves
1–2 packages Au Jus mix

Prepare the roast top by scoring the fat layer in a crisscross pattern to allow for better flavor absorption. Press beef bouillon granules into roast surface. Sprinkle garlic and seasoning salt over roast. Scatter oregano only on top of the roast.

Preheat oven to 325° F. Place roast on a suspended rack in a roasting pan. Prepare the Au Jus mix according to package directions and pour it into the roasting pan, under the roast. Make an aluminum foil tent to place over the top of the roast (to contain moisture as roast cooks). Make sure the foil does not rest on the roast; attaching it to the roasting pan works well.

Insert a meat thermometer or oven probe into the center of the roast so that the thermometer head does not touch the surface of the roast. (Be sure to prepare a hole in the foil tent to accommodate the thermometer, taking care that the foil does not come into contact with the thermometer.)

For medium-rare roast, cook to an internal temperature of 125°–135° F, allowing 15–20 minutes per pound cooking time. For medium roast, cook to an internal temperature of 135°–140° F, allowing 25–30 minutes per pound cook time.

IMPORTANT: The center of the roast will continue to cook after removal from the oven. Once cooked, the roast needs time to "rest" before cutting. Allow at least 15 minutes for a roast weighing up to 5 pounds. Roasts 6 pounds and over should rest for 25–30 minutes before carving.

Stuffed Turkey Breast

Yield: 8–10 servings | **Prep Time:** 35 minutes | **Bake Time:** 65 minutes
Rest Time: 10 minutes

When a whole turkey is too much but turkey at the table is a must, this moist stuffed turkey breast meets the need. Its presentation is as lovely as its taste is superb.

8 tablespoons unsalted butter

1 large yellow onion, diced

2 cups diced celery

1 fennel bulb, trimmed and diced (approximately 1½ cups)

2 tablespoons minced mixed fresh herbs (rosemary, sage, and thyme are a perfect combination)

⅓ cup minced fresh flat-leaf parsley

1½ teaspoons salt

¾ teaspoons freshly ground black pepper, to taste

1 box stuffing mix

3–3 ½ cups chicken stock, warmed, plus more if needed

2 4-pound boneless turkey breast halves, butterflied by your butcher and pounded to ½-inch thickness

Kitchen twine, for tying rolled roasts

2 tablespoons extra-virgin olive oil, divided between the 2 roasts

1 jar turkey gravy base, prepared according to package directions, for serving (or use homemade gravy)

Preheat oven to 425° F. In a large saucepan over medium heat, melt butter. Add onion, celery, and fennel; sauté, stirring occasionally, until soft and translucent, about 7 minutes. Add mixed fresh herbs, parsley, salt, and pepper; stir to combine. Transfer ingredients to a large bowl. Add stuffing mix and 3 cups of stock; stir to combine. Add more stock if needed to form a moist stuffing. Set aside.

Place 1 butterflied turkey breast on a work surface with long side nearest you. Season with salt and pepper. Mound 3 cups of stuffing running down center of breast, leaving a 1-inch border on each long side. Roll the long side nearest you over the stuffing to enclose, gently pressing on the filling, and roll to form a cylinder; do not roll too tightly or the filling will slip out through the ends. Using kitchen twine, tie the rolled turkey breast crosswise at 1-inch intervals.

Rub the outside of the breast with 1 tablespoon olive oil and season with salt and pepper. Place roast, rolled edge down, in large turkey roasting pan. Repeat process

with the other turkey breast half. (You may have some leftover stuffing.) Place remaining roast alongside first roast, also with rolled edge down. Roast turkey for 25 minutes at 425° F, then reduce oven temperature to 350° F. Continue roasting for about 40 minutes or until the skin is crisp and an instant-read thermometer inserted into the thickest part of the breasts registers 165° F.

Transfer turkey breasts to a carving board, cover loosely with aluminum foil, and let rest for 5–10 minutes. Slice into ½-inch slices, removing twine as you go. Serve immediately with your family's favorite gravy.

Salads

One of our ancient Sunset cookbooks says salads are one of the simplest and zestiest creations of the culinary arts. We have to agree. Salads provide leafy green freshness, often with crunchy fresh vegetables tossed in, enhanced and brought to splendor by a flavorful dressing. And we delight in how easy they are to make and how pretty they are to serve!

Citrus-Ambrosia Salad

Yield: 8 servings | **Prep Time:** 10 minutes | **Cook Time:** 3 minutes

Classic, diet-derailing ambrosia salad becomes a healthy ambrosia, thanks to trading a refreshing tart dressing made with citrus juices for the mayonnaise.

¾ cup unsweetened coconut flakes
1 15.5-ounce can citrus segments in juice, refrigerated
2 limes
¼ teaspoon salt
⅛ teaspoon coarsely ground black pepper
3 tablespoons extra-virgin olive oil
2 bags (5–6 ounces) mixed baby greens or spring mix with herbs

Preheat oven to 350° F. Place coconut in a single layer on a large jelly-roll pan. Toast 3 minutes or until golden. (Caution: coconut burns easily; check after 2 minutes.)

Drain citrus segments, reserving 1 tablespoon juice in large bowl. From limes, grate ½ teaspoon peel and squeeze 2 tablespoons juice; add to reserved citrus juice in bowl. Whisk in salt and pepper. Add oil in a thin, steady stream, whisking until well blended. Add greens to dressing; toss to coat. Arrange dressed greens on 8 chilled salad plates; top with citrus segments and toasted coconut.

Crab and Watermelon Napoleons

Yield: 4 servings | **Prep Time:** 10 minutes

Napoleons don't have to come from the bakery! These unique, summery entrées or sides consist of layers of creamy homemade dill crab salad and refreshing watermelon rounds.

2 cups cooked and flaked crab
⅔ cup mayonnaise
1½ tablespoons fresh snipped dill
12 watermelon rounds (approximately ½ inch thick)
4 sprigs of dill for garnish

In a medium bowl, mix crab, mayonnaise, and dill. Chill mixture until ready to build and serve Napoleons.

To serve, place a round of watermelon on a serving plate and top with a thin layer of crab salad. Top with another watermelon round and garnish with dill sprig. Repeat process to create 3 more Napoleons. Serve immediately.

BLT Cylinder Salad

Yield: 1 serving | **Prep Time:** 30 minutes

The presentation of this salad is unusual and fun. Depending on the size of the can, this can be a single serving or makes enough to feed a small crowd.

1 large plus 4 small butter lettuce leaves, washed and patted dry
2 slices from large tomato, ¼ inch thick
1 small avocado, peeled and thinly sliced
¼ cup feta or bleu cheese, crumbled
6 slices bacon, fried, drained and crumbled into small pieces
1 hard-cooked egg, sliced or crumbled, for salad
1 hard-cooked egg, sliced for garnish

Cut off both ends of a 28-ounce can. Wash and dry the can. You will use the can to create the cylinder shape of the salad. On a dinner plate, place lettuce leaves. Put the can on top of the lettuce. One ingredient category at a time, press each into the can, creating layers. Press firmly without smashing the salad ingredients. With your hand on top of the salad, remove can. Garnish with reserved egg.

This salad is best served with a creamy salad dressing such as Green Goddess or Ranch.

TIP: Cylinder Salad is easy to experiment with, so feel free to try various can sizes.

Mint-Infused Salad

Yield: 11 1-cup servings | **Prep Time:** 20 minutes

A mortar and pestle is used in this recipe to infuse fresh mint into sugar, which is then added to the prepared fruit. The dressing of mint-infused sugar brings out the flavors of each fruit without creating an overly sweet fruit salad—resulting in a truly unique salad that is one of our family favorites and first choice when hosting a brunch!

2 cups halved grapes
1 cup hulled and sliced strawberries
1 cup diced fresh pineapple
2 cups diced honeydew melon
1 cup diced cantaloupe
1 cup diced fresh grapefruit
1 cup blueberries
2 cups diced orange slices
2 tablespoons sugar
4 tablespoons minced fresh mint leaves

In a large bowl, combine all ingredients except mint and sugar. Using a mortar and pestle, grind minced mint and sugar together until well blended. Add minted sugar to fruit and lightly mix. Cover and chill salad at least 3 hours or overnight. Garnish with extra mint leaves if desired.

La Maison Salad

Yield: 4–6 servings | **Prep Time:** 20 minutes

This pleasant dinner salad goes well with everything. Served with crusty rolls, it makes the perfect light summer supper.

2 cups Romaine lettuce
2 cups cherry tomatoes
1 cup grated hard Swiss cheese
1½ cups slivered, lightly toasted almonds
⅓ cup grated Parmesan cheese
1 cup croutons
½ cup cooked bacon, cut in 2-inch pieces

DRESSING:
3 tablespoons lemon juice
½ teaspoon salt
½ cup extra-virgin olive oil
3 cloves garlic, minced
¼ teaspoon pepper

In a large bowl, toss lettuce, tomatoes, Swiss cheese, almonds, Parmesan cheese, croutons, and bacon; set aside. Prepare dressing by blending lemon juice, salt, oil, garlic, and pepper at high speed in a blender or food processor. Pour over salad, toss, and serve immediately.

TIP: Bacon can be quickly and easily cooked in a microwave by laying pieces atop a microwave-safe plate covered with a paper towel. Cover the bacon with another paper towel and cook on high for 2–3 minutes or until it reaches the preferred doneness.

Marinated Vegetable Salad

Yield: 8 servings | **Prep Time:** 20 minutes

Pair the convenience of a make-ahead dish with exquisite taste, and you have a salad that will become one of your hallmark dishes. This is such a great change from the usual three-bean salad and is perfect for picnics and parties!

2½ quarts water
3 tablespoons lemon juice
3 pounds small fresh mushrooms
2 carrots, thinly sliced
2 celery ribs, thinly sliced
½ medium bell pepper (any color), chopped
1 small red onion, chopped
1 tablespoon minced fresh parsley
½ cup sliced stuffed olives
1 2¼-ounce can sliced ripe olives, drained

DRESSING:
½ cup Italian salad dressing
⅓ cup red or white wine vinegar
1 large clove garlic, minced
½ teaspoon dried oregano

In a large saucepan, bring water and lemon juice to a boil. Add mushrooms and cook for 3 minutes, stirring occasionally. Drain; cool. In a large bowl, combine mushrooms, carrots, celery, bell pepper, onion, parsley, and olives. In a small bowl or jar with a tight-fitting lid, combine all dressing ingredients; shake or mix well. Pour over salad. Cover and refrigerate overnight.

Quinoa and Pear Salad

Yield: 4 servings | **Prep Time:** 15 minutes | **Cook Time:** 15 minutes

Here's a fresh idea to liven up a ho-hum salad. This light, vegan, packed-with-protein recipe is loaded with fresh green peas, toasted pecans, and succulent juicy pear.

1 cup quinoa
2 hefty handfuls baby spinach leaves, washed and drained
1 large ripe pear, washed, stemmed and cored, cut into pieces
½ cup fresh baby green peas
2 tablespoons fresh chopped parsley
¾ cup pecans or walnuts, pan-toasted and salted to taste
4 tablespoons extra-virgin olive oil
1½ tablespoons golden balsamic vinegar
2 tablespoons pure maple syrup
Salt, to taste
Pepper, to taste

Cook quinoa until tender, approximately 15 minutes. Let cool and set aside. In a large bowl, combine spinach, pear, peas, parsley, and nuts. In a blender, mix olive oil, vinegar, maple syrup, salt, and pepper. Add quinoa to salad ingredients; toss lightly. Pour dressing over salad and lightly toss one more time.

Strawberry Chicken Salad

Yield: 4 servings | **Prep Time:** 20 minutes

Salads are the meal of choice when the weather gets warm. Strawberries and chicken make an amazing duo in a salad that's substantial but not too heavy. You'll love how this unexpected combination tastes and will delight in how pretty it looks on your plate.

DRESSING

½ cup honey
½ cup red wine vinegar
4 teaspoons soy sauce
1 clove garlic, minced
⅛ teaspoon salt
Dash pepper

SALAD

1 pound boneless, skinless chicken breasts, cut into strips
1½ tablespoons butter
8 cups torn mixed salad greens
1 pint strawberries, sliced (more for garnish, if desired)
¼ cup thinly sliced purple onion
½ cup chopped, candied almond slivers

In a small bowl, combine dressing ingredients. In a large skillet, cook and stir chicken in butter until chicken is no longer pink; drain. Add ½ cup salad dressing and cook 1 minute longer. In a serving bowl, place salad greens; top with chicken, strawberries, onion, and nuts. Garnish with whole strawberries, if desired.

TIP: Knowing how to make candied nuts is a skill worth having. They add such sparkle to so many dishes—salads especially. To make candied slivered almonds, cook 1 cup almonds with 2 tablespoons sugar in a frying pan over medium heat, stirring constantly until sugar is dissolved and nuts are well coated. Spread nuts onto a cookie sheet to cool.

Sweet Potato Salad

Yield: 8–10 servings | **Prep Time:** 15 minutes plus chilling | **Cook Time:** 15–20 minutes plus cooling

While not a common potato salad in some parts of the country, sweet potato salad quickly becomes a favorite of those who try it. This new and healthy twist on potato salad is as tasty as it is pretty to look at.

2 pounds sweet potatoes
1½ cups mayonnaise
2 teaspoons Dijon mustard
½ teaspoon sea salt
5 hard-cooked eggs, chopped
1½ cups finely chopped celery
12 green onions, thinly sliced

Cut potatoes into quarters and place in a large saucepan; cover with water. Cover and boil gently until the potatoes can easily be pierced with the tip of a sharp knife—approximately 15–20 minutes. Drain. When potatoes are cool, peel and dice.

In a large bowl, combine mayonnaise, mustard, and salt. Stir in eggs, celery, and onions. Add potatoes; stir gently to mix. Cover and refrigerate 2–4 hours.

Smoked Cheddar and Grape Salad

Yield: 6 servings | **Prep Time:** 15 minutes

Smoked cheddar cheese is the unique element that takes this famous salad over the top. The smoky cheese pairs nicely with the tart apples, and the grapes round out the color spectrum, making this salad look as beautiful as it tastes.

½ cup mayonnaise
4 tablespoons sour cream
2 tablespoons fresh lemon juice
1 teaspoon sugar
1 cup cubed smoked cheddar cheese
4 Granny Smith or gala apples, cored, cut into ½-inch pieces
1½ cups very thinly sliced celery
1½ cups halved red seedless grapes
1 cup lightly chopped walnuts
Salt and pepper, to taste (if desired)
Romaine lettuce leaves

In a large bowl, whisk mayonnaise, sour cream, lemon juice, and sugar. Add cheese cubes, apples, celery, grapes, and walnuts. Toss well with dressing. Season with salt and pepper, if desired. Arrange washed Romaine lettuce leaves on a platter or in a large salad bowl and spoon the salad over the leaves.

Spiced Pecan Salad with Lemon Dressing

Yield: 8 servings | **Prep Time:** 30 minutes | **Cook Time:** 25 minutes

Spicy pecans and Greek yogurt create a flavor combination that's hard to beat. We get lots of requests for this decades-old salad when we ask the family what we should have for dinner!

SALAD

2 heads Romaine lettuce
2 Gala apples, peeled and sliced, covered
    with lemon juice to prevent browning
4 ounces grated white Cheddar cheese
1 tablespoon minced chives
½–1 cup spiced pecans (recipe follows)
Honey-Yogurt Dressing (recipe follows)

In a large salad bowl, combine all ingredients except dressing; lightly toss until well combined. Serve immediately with honey-yogurt dressing.

SPICED PECANS

1 egg white
2 cups whole or halved pecans
¼ cup sugar
½ teaspoon cinnamon
¼ teaspoon cayenne pepper
¼ teaspoon salt

Preheat oven to 325° F. Whisk egg white until foamy, stir in pecans, and toss until well coated. Combine sugar, cinnamon, cayenne pepper, and salt. Pour spice mixture over pecans and toss until coated. Spread on cookie sheet lined with parchment paper. Cook 20–25 minutes, stirring frequently.

HONEY-YOGURT DRESSING

3 tablespoons freshly squeezed lemon juice
    (not bottled)
Zest of one lemon
¾ cup plain Greek yogurt
2 tablespoons honey
½ teaspoon salt

Combine all ingredients and blend well. Store in a covered container in the refrigerator until ready to use.

Side Dishes

In a way, the term *side dish* implies an extra added attraction. But over time it's come to be a mainstay of a well-rounded menu. The beautiful thing about many of our side dishes is how versatile they are. Pair them with a hearty whole-grain bread or a fresh salad, and they make a pleasant meal in and of themselves!

Rice Verde

Yield: 4 servings | **Prep Time:** 10 minutes | **Cook Time:** 25 minutes

A traditional favorite on any Mexican menu, this easy and pretty side dish also goes well with baked beans.

2 cups chicken stock
1 jalapeño pepper
1–1½ cups cilantro leaves
½ teaspoon salt
2 tablespoons extra-virgin olive oil
1 cup onion, finely chopped
4 cloves garlic, chopped
1 cup Jasmine or other long-grain rice
¼ teaspoon black pepper

In a blender, combine chicken stock, jalapeño pepper, cilantro, and salt. Blend until ingredients are smooth.

In a medium saucepan over medium heat, sauté onion in olive oil until soft, approximately 2 minutes. Add garlic and sauté for 1 minute. Add the rice, black pepper, and cilantro puree; cover and bring to a boil. Reduce heat to low and continue cooking until the liquid is absorbed and rice is tender, about 20 minutes.

Bandito Beans

Yield: 6 servings | **Prep Time:** 15 minutes | **Cook Time:** 4 hours 10 minutes

Combining a variety of beans along with chopped onion and traditional seasonings creates a rich, savory baked bean that we consider a blue ribbon winner! This easy recipe is one of our favorites for summertime entertaining.

16 ounces bacon, divided
1 pound ground beef
¾ cup chopped onion
2 12-ounce cans pinto beans, drained and rinsed
1 15-ounce can black beans, drained and rinsed
1 15-ounce can white beans, drained and rinsed
2 15-ounce cans baked beans with pork
1 cup barbecue sauce
1 cup ketchup
1 cup brown sugar

In a large, deep skillet over medium-high heat, cook the bacon until evenly brown. Drain on paper towels, crumble, and set aside. Drain bacon fat from the skillet.

Using the same skillet, cook the ground beef and onion over medium heat, stirring until the meat is no longer pink, 5–7 minutes. Drain.

Transfer the ground beef to a slow-cooker. Add all the beans, 1 cup crumbled bacon, barbecue sauce, ketchup, and brown sugar; stir to blend well. Cover and cook in a slow-cooker on HIGH for 4 hours. Top each serving with remaining crumbled bacon.

Peppered Corn Fritters
Yield: 13–14 fritters | **Prep Time:** 20 minutes

Cumin complements the corn and peppers in these pretty fritters. They're a nice alternative to rice or potatoes and sit well alongside a variety of meat entrées.

1¼ cups fresh or frozen corn, thawed
½ cup finely chopped sweet red pepper
½ cup finely chopped green onion
2 teaspoons chopped fresh parsley
1¼ cups flour
2 teaspoons baking powder
½ teaspoon ground cumin
½ teaspoon salt
¼ teaspoon pepper
1¼ cups milk
2 tablespoons extra-virgin olive oil
Canola oil for frying

In a medium bowl, combine corn, red pepper, onions, and parsley. In a separate bowl, combine flour, baking powder, cumin, salt, and pepper; stir into corn mixture. Gradually add milk, stirring until blended. In a skillet over medium heat, heat 4 tablespoons oil. Form mixture into 13–14 fritters and cook, 3 or 4 at a time, for 2 minutes on each side or until golden brown. Repeat with remaining batter, adding more oil as needed.

Oven-Baked Asparagus

Yield: 4 servings | **Prep Time:** 15 minutes | **Cook Time:** 12–15 minutes

Asparagus is one of the traditional harbingers of spring, and this easy side dish is such a great way to celebrate the passing of winter, the wonderful hope of warmer days, and the arrival of fresh fruits and vegetables. Considered the king of vegetables, asparagus is well worth waiting for!

1 bunch thin asparagus spears, washed well and trimmed
3 tablespoons olive oil
2½ tablespoons grated Parmesan cheese
1 clove garlic, minced
1 teaspoon sea salt
½ teaspoon ground black pepper

Preheat oven to 425° F. Place asparagus in a large mixing bowl; drizzle spears with olive oil. Toss to coat the spears, then sprinkle with cheese, garlic, salt, and pepper.

Arrange asparagus onto a baking sheet in a single layer. Bake until just tender, 12–15 minutes, depending on thickness of spears.

TIPS FOR BUYING AND PREPARING ASPARAGUS:
—Look for spears that are uniform in size with tight, healthy tips that are not crushed.
—Choose asparagus that has been kept chilled/on ice while on display.
—Use asparagus as soon as possible after purchasing, as it deteriorates quickly. Storing it upright in a small amount of water in your refrigerator will help preserve it longer.
—Cut or snap off the woody ends of stalks prior to cooking.

TIPS FOR COOKING ASPARAGUS:
—The best asparagus is cooked just enough to make it tender, but still with a touch of crispness and a bright green color.
—If serving hot, remove the asparagus from the heat slightly before it is done, as it will continue to cook after it is removed from the heat.
—If serving cold, cook until done and immediately stop the cooking by rinsing in cold water.

Cheese and Garlic Spread

Yield: 8 servings | **Prep Time:** 5 minutes | **Cook Time:** 3 minutes

This fantastic spread jazzes up any bread, but especially a crusty loaf of French bread. Sometimes all we want for dinner is a hearty salad and bread adorned with this wonderful spread—it's that good!

½ cup butter, softened
¼ cup mayonnaise
½ cup grated cheese
1 teaspoon garlic powder
1 tablespoon dried parsley flakes

In a small bowl, mix all ingredients until well blended. Refrigerate any leftovers (good luck with that!).

Basic Potato Latkes

Yield: Approximately 24 latkes | **Prep Time:** 20 minutes | **Cook Time:** 20 minutes

Potato latkes are pan-fried in oil until golden, then served with side dishes of sour cream and applesauce. While usually considered to be part of a traditional Hanukkah celebration, this beautiful and tasty dish ought to be enjoyed all year!

1 yellow onion
1½ teaspoons coarse salt
¼ teaspoon freshly ground pepper
2 large eggs
⅓ cup matzo meal
4 large Russet potatoes, peeled
Peanut oil, for frying
Pink applesauce and sour cream for serving,
   if desired

Using a food processor, grate onion. In a large bowl, combine onion, salt, pepper, and eggs; stir until incorporated. Stir in matzo meal until mixture is smooth. Use the food processor to grate the potatoes. Add potatoes to the onion and egg mixture. Mix well until potatoes are evenly coated.

Fill a large, heavy-bottomed skillet with approximately ½ inch of oil. Place skillet over medium heat until oil just reaches the smoking point. (To test, drop a small bit of batter into the skillet; the oil should sizzle upon contact.)

Working in batches so as not to crowd skillet, carefully spoon approximately 2 tablespoons batter into oil for each pancake. Lightly tamp down to flatten. Cook until golden, 2–3 minutes on each side, turning once. Using a slotted spatula, transfer cooked latkes to a paper-towel-lined wire rack for draining. Repeat process with remaining batter. Serve immediately with applesauce and sour cream, if desired.

TIPS: To prevent the potatoes from discoloring too much, peel and grate them just before using.

When making latkes, there's no need to squeeze the moisture out of the grated potatoes (a messy and labor-intensive process at best). Just stir the mixture right before you form it into pancakes, and incorporate the liquid from the bottom of the bowl as you work. You may have as much as ½ cup liquid left over after all the pancakes have been formed.

VARIATION: SWEET POTATO LATKES
Yield: Approximately 24 latkes |
Prep Time: 20 minutes |
Cook Time: 20 minutes

While classic latkes consist of grated potatoes, onions, and eggs, it's delicious to include other vegetables, such as sweet potatoes or spinach.

3 green onions, thinly sliced
2 large eggs
⅓ cup all-purpose flour
1½ teaspoons coarse salt
¼ teaspoon ground ginger
⅛ teaspoon ground cardamom
¼ teaspoon freshly ground pepper
3 sweet potatoes, peeled
3 small Yukon gold potatoes, peeled
Peanut oil, for frying
Pink applesauce and sour cream for serving,
    if desired

In a large bowl, combine onions and eggs. Add flour, salt, ginger, cardamom, and pepper; stir until mixture is smooth. In a food processor, grate sweet potatoes and Yukon gold potatoes; add to egg and flour mixture. Toss until combined and potatoes are evenly coated.

Fill a large, heavy-bottomed skillet with approximately ½ inch of oil. Place skillet over medium heat until oil just reaches the smoking point. (To test, drop a small bit of batter into the skillet; the oil should sizzle upon contact.)

Working in batches so as not to crowd skillet, carefully spoon approximately 2 tablespoons batter into oil for each pancake. Lightly tamp down to flatten. Cook until golden,
2–3 minutes on each side, turning once. Using a slotted spatula, transfer cooked latkes to a paper-towel-lined wire rack for draining. Repeat process with remaining batter. Serve immediately with applesauce and sour cream, if desired.

TIP: Watch these closely while frying; the sugar in the sweet potatoes causes them to brown quickly.

Ultra-Loaded Potatoes

Yield: 10–12 servings | **Prep Time:** 15 minutes | **Bake Time:** 45 minutes

From the repertoire of Alice's son, professional cook and chef Paul Fulton, comes a revved-up approach to a classic theme—loaded potatoes. It's not often you'll find a mashed potato that wouldn't sit better under gravy, but this is it.

5 pounds potatoes
8 ounces cream cheese, softened
4 ounces sour cream
¼ cup butter, softened and divided
½ teaspoon onion salt
1 cup finely sliced green onions
¾ cup cooked, crumbled bacon
1 cup grated sharp cheddar cheese
Dried chopped parsley, for garnish

Peel, cube, and cook potatoes in salted water. While potatoes are cooking, in a medium bowl beat cream cheese, 3 tablespoons butter, and onion salt. Set aside. In another bowl, mix onions, bacon, and cheese. Once potatoes are cooked and drained, mash the potatoes and beat in the cream cheese mixture. Fold in the onion, bacon, and cheese mixture. Transfer to a serving bowl and garnish with remaining 1 tablespoon butter and sprinkles of dried parsley.

TIP: For extra fiber, minerals, color, and taste, consider cooking the potatoes with the skins on and mashing the skins into the rest of the ingredients.

Guacamole Olé

Yield: Approximately 1½ cups | **Prep Time:** 20 minutes

Avocados are a nutrient-dense, versatile fruit that can be eaten alone or used in a variety of tasty recipes—from soups to salads to smoothies to this no-fail guacamole. "Olé!" is what you'll hear when serving this family-favorite dish.

3 avocados, peeled and halved
2 limes, juiced
½ teaspoon salt
½ teaspoon ground cumin
¾ cup red onion, minced
½ to 1 jalapeño pepper, seeded and minced
2–3 large Roma tomatoes, finely diced
1 packed tablespoon cilantro, chopped
1–2 cloves garlic, minced

In a large bowl, mash avocado, lime juice, salt, and cumin. Fold in onions, jalapeño pepper, tomatoes, cilantro, and garlic. Serve immediately.

TIP: For a healthy alternative to Ranch or other standard dressings, add a little sour cream to this guacamole and use atop a green salad!

Yellow Squash Casserole

Yield: 8 servings | **Prep Time:** 20 minutes | **Bake Time:** 45 minutes

Hearty and satisfying, this casserole has a nice texture because the squash rind stays just slightly firm.

2 pounds yellow crookneck squash, sliced
3 eggs, lightly beaten
½ cup heavy cream
¼ cup butter, melted and divided
1 cup thinly sliced celery
1 cup finely chopped onion
1 teaspoon salt
½ teaspoon pepper
1½ cups shredded cheddar cheese, divided
9 slices bacon, cooked and crumbled

Preheat oven to 400° F. Cook squash in boiling, salted water until tender. Drain well and mash. Transfer squash to a large bowl and mix in eggs, cream, and 2 tablespoons melted butter. Sauté celery and onion in remaining 2 tablespoons butter until vegetables are transparent. Add vegetables to the squash; mix in salt, pepper, and ¾ cup cheese. Pour into a 9 x 13-inch baking dish. Sprinkle with remaining cheese and top with cooked bacon. Bake for 45 minutes.

Zucchini Gratin

Yield: 8–10 servings | **Prep Time:** 40 minutes | **Bake Time:** 20 minutes

The cheese and nutmeg are the stars in this recipe. The versatile flavor combinations work beautifully with cauliflower as well. This dish is a hit with company, as a side dish, or as the focus of the meal.

6 tablespoons butter, plus extra for topping
3 large yellow onions, cut in halves and sliced
2 pounds zucchini (about 4 zucchini), sliced
    ¼ inch thick
2 teaspoons kosher salt
1 teaspoon ground black pepper
¼ teaspoon grated nutmeg
2 tablespoons flour
1 cup hot milk
¾ cup Gruyère cheese, divided
½ cup bread crumbs
Bacon, cooked and crumbled, for garnish
    (optional)

Preheat oven to 400° F. In a medium saucepan, melt 6 tablespoons butter and cook onions over low heat for 20 minutes, or until tender but not browned. Add zucchini and cook, covered, for 10 minutes, or until tender. Add the salt, pepper, and nutmeg and cook uncovered for 5 minutes. Stir in flour; add hot milk and cook over low heat for a few minutes until mixture becomes a sauce. Pour mixture into an 8 x 11 x 2-inch dish. Combine bread crumbs with Gruyère cheese and sprinkle over zucchini mixture. Dot with 1 tablespoon butter cut into small bits. Bake for 20 minutes or until bubbly and nicely browned. Garnish with cooked, crumbled bacon if desired.

TIP: Swiss cheese can be used instead of the Gruyère cheese because the flavors are so similar.

Spicy Sweet Potatoes

Yield: 8 servings | **Prep Time:** 10 minutes | **Cook Time:** 45 minutes

This recipe is not only good for you, it's easy to prepare. Sweet potatoes are a perfect food for stabilizing blood sugar, an added bonus to such a delicious recipe.

2 medium sweet potatoes, peeled and cut into 1-inch cubes (approximately 4 cups)
2 medium yams, peeled and cut into 1-inch cubes (approximately 4 cups)
3 tablespoons extra-virgin olive oil
3 tablespoons brown sugar
1 teaspoon chili powder
1 teaspoon salt
½ teaspoon pepper

Preheat oven to 400° F. In a gallon-size plastic zip-top bag, toss cut sweet potatoes and yams in oil. In a small bowl, combine remaining ingredients; add to bag. Toss, coating potatoes and yams well. Transfer potatoes and yams to an oiled 9 x 13-inch pan. Bake uncovered for 40 minutes or until potatoes and yams are tender, stirring every 15 minutes.

Twice-Baked Asparagus Potato

Yield: 4 servings | **Prep Time:** 10 minutes
Bake Time: 65 minutes to 1 hour 25 minutes

What happens when you combine two flavor favorites—asparagus and bacon—in this delicious twist on a twice-baked potato? Nothing short of tastebud heaven!

4 medium baking potatoes
Olive oil, for coating potatoes
Kosher salt
1 tablespoon milk
½ cup sour cream
1 teaspoon onion salt
½ teaspoon garlic powder
⅛ teaspoon pepper
1 pound fresh asparagus, cut into 1-inch
    pieces and cooked
4–5 bacon strips, cooked and crumbled
1 cup shredded sharp cheddar cheese

Preheat oven to 400° F. Scrub potatoes well; dry and coat with olive oil. Sprinkle with kosher salt. Place potatoes directly on the top rack of your oven (place a baking sheet on the bottom rack to catch any drips) and bake for 45–60 minutes or until potatoes are soft.

Cut a thin slice off the long side of each potato and discard. Carefully scoop out pulp while leaving shell intact. In a mixing bowl, mash pulp with milk, sour cream, onion salt, garlic powder, and pepper until smooth. Fold in asparagus pieces and crumbled bacon. Stuff shells; place in a shallow, ungreased baking dish. Sprinkle with cheese. Return to the oven for 20–25 minutes or until potatoes are heated through.

TIP: Parboiled potatoes need less baking time and result in a fluffier texture. Prior to baking, boil potatoes for 10 minutes. Remove potatoes from water and bake in a preheated oven for approximately 35 minutes or until tender.

Soup, Stew, and Chowder

Soup, stew, and chowder—they fill a home with enticing aromas that bring hope to those who are eagerly waiting for dinner. Whether you use your slow-cooker or a simple soup pot, there's nothing like a bowl of hot goodness to settle in to on a cold day!

Black Bean Soup

Yield: 6–8 servings | **Prep Time:** 10 minutes | **Cook Time:** 4–5 hours

This is a hearty and delicious meatless meal. Serve with chips, sour cream, and grated cheese, and you have true comfort food.

1 15½-ounce can red kidney beans, drained and rinsed
1 15½-ounce can black beans
1 15¼-ounce can whole-kernel corn
1 14½-ounce can Italian- or Mexican-style tomatoes
1 4-ounce can chopped mild green chilies
1 teaspoon salt
1 teaspoon chili powder
½ teaspoon cumin
Pepper, to taste
1 medium onion, finely chopped
2 cloves garlic, minced
1–2 carrots, diced

Place all ingredients in slow-cooker. Cook on HIGH for 4–5 hours or on LOW for 8–10 hours.

Creamy Chicken Stew

Yield: 8 servings | **Prep Time:** 30 minutes | **Cook Time:** 4 hours

This delightful and filling stew can be frozen into individual portions for quick and easy meals later on. It also works well with leftover turkey, so keep this handy during the holidays.

1 pound fresh mushrooms, chopped

½ cup finely chopped shallots

½ cup water

4 cups fat-free chicken broth

½ cup celery, chopped

1 cup fresh zucchini, chopped

1 cup carrots, sliced

1 teaspoon fresh thyme leaves

1 teaspoon fresh rosemary, finely chopped

3 bay leaves

2 pounds boneless, skinless chicken thighs, trimmed and cut into bite-size chunks

2 tablespoons cornstarch

¼ cup water

1 12-ounce can evaporated milk

2 tablespoons lemon juice

1 teaspoon salt

½ teaspoon pepper

1½ cups frozen green peas, rinsed under cold water to thaw

½ cup chopped fresh parsley

In a 5- to 6-quart Dutch oven, combine mushrooms, shallots, and ½ cup water. Cover and cook on high heat, stirring often, for approximately 3–4 minutes. Uncover and cook, stirring often, until the mushrooms are lightly browned, 8–10 minutes. Add broth, celery, zucchini, carrots, thyme, rosemary, and bay leaves; bring to a boil.

In a 5- to 6-quart slow-cooker, place chicken. Turn heat to HIGH. Carefully pour in the vegetable mixture. Cover and cook until the chicken is very tender, approximately 3½–4 hours.

Transfer the chicken and vegetables to a large bowl and discard bay leaves. Skim fat and pour the juices into the previously used Dutch oven. Bring to a boil over high heat. Boil until reduced to 2 cups, 15–20 minutes. In a small bowl, mix cornstarch with ¼ cup water; add to the pan of juices and cook, stirring, until slightly thickened. Add the

evaporated milk and lemon juice; stir until boiling. Return the chicken and vegetables to the sauce in the Dutch oven and heat through. Season with salt and pepper, if desired. Just before serving, stir in peas and parsley.

TIP: Raw chicken is much easier to cut when slightly frozen.

Chicken and Wild Rice Soup

Yield: 8 cups | **Prep Time:** 10 minutes | **Cook Time:** 15 minutes

Soup's ready in 25 minutes when you use an instant wild rice mix and a rotisserie chicken from the supermarket. Everyone who tried this thought it was one of the best soups they've ever had. This 100 percent approval rating, along with it being tasty, quick, and simple, makes it one of our standards for wintertime cooking.

6 cups water
6 chicken bouillon cubes
1 package instant wild rice mix
¾ cup thinly sliced carrots
½ cup thinly sliced celery
¼ cup chopped onion
1½ cups roasted chicken, cut in bite-size pieces
2 10¾-ounce cans cream of chicken soup, undiluted

In a Dutch oven or large saucepan, bring water and bouillon to a boil. Add rice packet and enclosed seasoning. Add vegetables and chicken. Boil 10 minutes, stirring continually. Add undiluted cream of chicken soup to mixture. Stir another 5 minutes until cream of chicken soup is thoroughly incorporated.

Cream of Chicken Soup

Yield: Approximately 3 cups concentrated soup | **Prep Time:** 20 minutes

While most of us are interested in making our meals more healthy, there are just a few things we don't want to give up—and canned cream-of-anything soups qualify. Don't you agree? That said, you'll be excited to see this recipe for your OWN cream of chicken soup substitute—a healthy version with no MSG, fillers, preservatives, or mystery ingredients. Life is good!

1½ cups chicken stock, divided
½ teaspoon onion powder
¼ teaspoon garlic powder
1 clove garlic, finely chopped
1 teaspoon finely chopped onion
1¾ cups milk, divided
1 teaspoon butter
¼ teaspoon salt
¼ teaspoon black pepper
½ cup all-purpose flour

In a medium saucepan, combine 2 tablespoons chicken stock, onion powder, garlic powder, garlic clove, and chopped onion; cook and stir over medium-low heat until onion and garlic are soft, about 3 minutes. Add remaining stock and ¾ cup milk to pan; add butter; whisk in salt and pepper. Bring mixture to a boil, reduce heat, and simmer for 1–2 minutes. In a small bowl, whisk remaining 1 cup milk and flour until smooth, then whisk it into the hot stock mixture. Whisking continuously to avoid lumps, cook until soup thickens and almost comes to a boil.

To use as a soup, thin with equal parts milk and chicken stock. Use as is in casseroles and any other recipe calling for condensed cream of chicken soup.

Uptown Ham Chowder

Yield: 10 servings or 2 quarts | **Prep Time:** 10 minutes | **Cook Time:** 30 minutes

This full-flavored, comforting dish is a tasty way to use leftover ham and vegetables. The Gouda cheese adds a special and unexpected touch.

¾ cup chopped onion
½ cup finely chopped celery
1 cup frozen mixed vegetables
2 tablespoons butter
¼ cup all-purpose flour
1 envelope Ranch salad dressing mix
2 cups milk
2 cups half-and-half
2 cups leftover or frozen hash brown potatoes (best cut in cubes)
½ cup frozen white corn
2 cups fully cooked ham, cut in cubes
1 teaspoon minced fresh thyme or ¼ teaspoon dried thyme
½ teaspoon pepper
1½ cups shredded smoked Gouda cheese

In a large saucepan, sauté the onion, celery, and mixed vegetables in butter until crisp-tender. Stir in flour and dressing mix until blended; gradually stir in milk and half-and-half. Bring mixture to a boil; cook and stir for 2 minutes or until thickened.

Add the potatoes, corn, ham, thyme, and pepper. Bring to a boil. Reduce heat; simmer uncovered for 8–10 minutes to allow flavors to meld. Add cheese, stirring until melted and well blended.

Slow-Cooker Squash Soup

Yield: 4 servings | **Prep Time:** 35 minutes | **Cook Time:** 8 hours

Looking for a healthy, satisfying, and unusual way to use up that abundance of garden-fresh squash? Here's your answer. Pair this with fresh crusty rolls and a tossed salad, and dinner is served!

3 tablespoons extra-virgin olive oil
1 medium onion, thinly sliced
2 cloves garlic, sliced
2 tablespoons tomato paste
¼ teaspoon red pepper flakes
½ cup water
1½ cups dried garbanzo beans, rinsed
1 pound butternut squash, peeled, seeded, and cut into large pieces
1 bunch Swiss chard, leaves and stems separated and roughly chopped
1 piece Parmesan cheese rind, plus grated Parmesan for topping
2 teaspoons Kosher salt
Freshly ground pepper, to taste
7 cups water
6 slices cooked bacon, crumbled
Crusty bread and lemon wedges, for serving

In a large skillet over medium-high heat, heat olive oil. Add the onion and garlic and cook until soft and golden brown, approximately 4–5 minutes. Stir in the tomato paste and red pepper flakes and cook 1 minute. Stir in ½ cup water, scraping up any browned bits. Transfer the contents of the skillet to a 6-quart slow-cooker.

To the slow-cooker add garbanzo beans, squash, chard stems (not the leaves), Parmesan rind, salt, pepper, and 7 cups water. Stir, then cover and cook on LOW for 8 hours. Just before serving, lift cooker lid and stir in the chard leaves and crumbled bacon bits; cover and continue cooking 10 more minutes. Season with more salt and pepper, if desired, and stir to break up the squash. Discard the Parmesan rind. Ladle the soup into bowls; top with the grated Parmesan cheese. Serve with bread and lemon wedges.

Fresh Basil and Tomato Soup

Yield: 6 servings | **Prep Time:** 30 minutes | **Cook Time:** 30 minutes

Who doesn't love a hot bowl of soup on a cold day? The fresh tomatoes and basil give this recipe a divine, garden-goodness taste.

1 tablespoon olive oil
1 cup chopped onion
2 cloves garlic, minced
8 large fresh tomatoes
½ cup chopped carrot
¼ cup chopped celery
1 14.5-ounce can vegetable or chicken broth
1 teaspoon salt
½ teaspoon dried thyme
½ teaspoon freshly ground black pepper
1 tablespoon fresh minced basil

In a large Dutch oven over medium-high heat, heat oil. Sauté onion and garlic in olive oil until onion is tender. Add tomatoes and cook for 20 minutes. Add carrot, celery, broth, and seasonings; cook another 10 minutes. Let soup cool 10 minutes. Pour cooled ingredients, a few cups at a time, into a food processor and puree. Continue until all soup is pureed to desired consistency.

Zucchini Cheese Soup

Yield: 8 servings | **Prep Time:** 15 Minutes | **Cook Time:** 20 minutes

This is yet another way to be a Zucchini Houdini by using up the harvest from those prolific zucchini plants. This creamy, Southwest soup would make the perfect ending to a chilly fall day.

2 medium zucchini
1 medium onion
½ tablespoon dried parsley or 1 tablespoon
    fresh parsley, minced
1 teaspoon dried basil
⅓ cup butter
⅓ cup all-purpose flour
1 teaspoon salt
½ teaspoon pepper
3 cups water
3 chicken bouillon cubes (Mexican tomato-
    based bouillon is a good substitute)
1 teaspoon lemon juice
4 large Roma tomatoes, finely diced
1 4-ounce can mild green chilies
1 12-ounce can evaporated milk
1 15.25-ounce can whole-kernel corn,
    drained
¼ cup grated Parmesan cheese
2 cups shredded cheddar cheese

In a large soup pot, sauté zucchini, onion, parsley, and basil in butter until tender. Stir in flour, salt, and pepper. Gradually stir in water. Add bouillon and lemon juice; mix well and bring to a boil; cook and stir for 2 minutes. Add tomatoes, green chilies, milk, and corn; return mixture to a boil. Reduce heat; cover and simmer for 10 minutes. Add cheeses just before serving, and stir until cheeses are melted.

Desserts

So often our families sit down to our homemade, lovingly crafted dinners, only to ask before the first bite, "Hey, what's for dessert?" There's no getting around it—for most folks, dessert is the favorite course of a meal. Knowing this, we've combined ingredients in unusual ways, given family favorites some creative presentations, and invented our own recipes for some desserts we think are truly "to die for."

Orangesicle Pie

Yield: 16 servings (2 pies) | **Prep Time:** 15 minutes | **Bake Time:** 12 minutes

This tantalizing twist on a tried-and-true favorite, the Orange Julius, now shows up in a pie! This is so good, you'll be glad this recipe makes two pies!

1 8-ounce package cream cheese, softened
1 pint heavy whipping cream, whipped to stiff peaks
½ cup orange juice concentrate, thawed
1 4-ounce box instant vanilla pudding mix
1 3-ounce box orange-flavored gelatin
Oat-Nut Crust (recipe follows)

In a medium bowl, blend cream cheese and whipped cream well. Add juice concentrate and beat until very creamy. Stir in dry pudding mix and dry gelatin mix; blend well. Divide filling between crusts; chill at least 3 hours before serving.

OAT-NUT CRUST

1½ cups flour
1 cup quick-cooking oats
1 cup chopped nuts
½ cup unsweetened shredded coconut
4 tablespoons sugar
½ teaspoon salt
1 cup melted butter

Preheat oven to 375° F. Thoroughly mix all ingredients. Press into two 9-inch pie plates. Bake crusts for approximately 12 minutes or until golden brown. Cool crusts well before filling.

Chocolate Fudge Dream Cake
Yield: 8 big slices | **Prep Time:** 20 minutes | **Bake Time:** 30 minutes

This extra-special cake was first prepared for a potluck by Megan Stapley, Jeanne's sixteen-year-old granddaughter. She started with two 8-inch cake rounds sliced in half to make four layers. Each layer was mounded with Cloud Nine Frosting. This dessert won raves and applause from everyone who tried it, and Megan's baking career was launched.

Megan's mother, Jill, toyed with the idea of covering the sides of this already-amazing cake with her grandma's fudge frosting. Not only did the fudge frosting make the cake more decadent, it added to its beauty. And thus was born the now-famous Chocolate Fudge Dream Cake.

¾ cup butter, softened
2 cups sugar
¾ cup Dutch cocoa
2 large eggs
1 tablespoon baking soda
¾ teaspoon salt
2 teaspoons vanilla extract
1 cup buttermilk
3 cups flour
1 cup hot water

Preheat oven to 350° F. Butter and dust two 9-inch round cake pans (see **Tip**). In a large bowl, cream butter and sugar. Add cocoa and eggs; mix well. Add baking soda, salt, and vanilla. Alternately blend in the buttermilk, flour, and hot water. The batter should be smooth. Bake for 30–35 minutes or until an inserted toothpick comes out clean. Allow cake to completely cool. When cake is cool, evenly slice each layer in half, creating 4 round layers. Frost with

Cloud Nine Frosting and Chocolate Fudge Frosting, following directions below.

TIP: After buttering your cake pans, dust with sugar rather than flour. This gives the cake a nice sugary texture that makes it easy to frost. Another option is to dust the buttered pans with cocoa powder.

CLOUD NINE FROSTING
8 ounces cream cheese, softened
¾ cup brown sugar
1 teaspoon vanilla extract
Dash salt
2 cups heavy whipping cream

In a medium bowl, cream the cream cheese, brown sugar, vanilla, and salt until smooth. In a separate medium bowl, beat the whipping cream until stiff peaks form. Fold the whipped cream into the cream cheese mixture.

CHOCOLATE FUDGE FROSTING

1 cup sugar
⅓ cup milk
5 tablespoons butter
1 cup semi-sweet chocolate chips

In a medium saucepan, combine sugar, milk, and butter; bring to a boil, stirring constantly. Remove from heat and add chocolate chips. With a wire whisk, beat until creamy and slightly cooled (approximately 10 minutes).

To frost the cake: Place the first cake layer on a decorative serving plate or cake stand and generously frost with Cloud Nine Frosting. Repeat with the next two layers, generously frosting the top of each. Place the fourth layer on top and leave unfrosted, but make sure you reserve enough Cloud Nine Frosting to later frost the top.

Smooth Chocolate Fudge Frosting around the sides of all four layers of cake. Finish frosting the cake by adding the remaining Cloud Nine Frosting to the top layer of cake, mounding it in the middle.

TIP: A perfect finishing touch is to grate some shavings of chocolate bar over the top of the cake, around the sides of the cake, and on the edges of the cake stand.

Blue Ribbon Cherry Pie

Yield: 3 cups pie filling | **Prep Time:** 10 minutes | **Baking Time:** 45 minutes

Is there anything that says "Let's eat!" better than a homemade pie? This filling rivals even Grandma's cherry pie!

1⅓ cups sugar
½ teaspoon almond extract
⅓ cup flour
2 tablespoons butter, melted
1 14.5-ounce can pitted tart red cherries, drained well

Mix all ingredients and store in the refrigerator for up to 2 days. When ready to make the pie, remove filling from the refrigerator and allow it to come to room temperature. Line a pie plate with Jeanne's No-Fail Pie Crust (recipe and step-by-step instructions follow) and top with second layer of crust. Seal edges, trim excess crust, and slit top to allow for steam to escape as pie bakes.

While many pie recipes call for baking at high temperatures, we've found that baking at a moderate 350° F results in a well-done pie without a scorched pie crust. Bake for 45 minutes or until crust is golden brown.

JEANNE'S NO-FAIL PIE CRUST

4 cups flour
1¾ cups butter-flavored shortening
1 tablespoon sugar
2 teaspoons salt
1 tablespoon vinegar
1 egg
½ cup ice water

In a large bowl and using a pastry blender or fork, mix flour, shortening, sugar, and salt until the mixture resembles coarse crumbs. In a small bowl, combine vinegar, egg, and water; mix well. Add wet ingredients to the flour mixture and blend quickly. Be careful not to overwork the dough; mix just until liquid is absorbed by the flour mixture. Refrigerate at least 15 minutes before rolling. This dough can be divided into individual crust portions, wrapped, and frozen for later use.

Birthday Party Ice Cream Cake Roll

Yield: 12–16 servings | **Prep Time:** 20 minutes | **Freeze Time:** 3–4 hours

Ice cream and cake, all rolled into one—literally! This recipe provides a festive and unique birthday cake experience for all involved. The Dutch cocoa adds a deep and satisfying chocolate flavor to the cake that any chocolate-lover will truly appreciate.

⅓ cup powdered sugar, plus more for final dusting
1 cup unsweetened Dutch cocoa powder, divided
⅓ cup cake flour
2 tablespoons cornstarch
½ teaspoon baking soda
½ teaspoon baking powder
½ teaspoon salt
4 large eggs, separated
¾ cup sugar, divided
½ gallon cherry ice cream, softened

Preheat oven to 350° F. In a small bowl, combine ⅓ cup powdered sugar with ⅓ cup cocoa powder. Line a 15 x 10-inch jelly roll pan with waxed paper. Butter the paper and dust with powdered sugar and cocoa mixture. Tap off extra mixture and reserve for later.

In a large bowl, combine flour, remaining ⅔ cup cocoa powder, cornstarch, baking soda, baking powder, and salt; mix well.

In another large bowl, beat egg yolks and ¼ cup sugar until fluffy. In a small bowl, using clean beaters, beat egg whites until foamy. Gradually add remaining ½ cup sugar, beating until stiff (but not dry) peaks form. Fold ⅓ of the beaten egg whites into the yolk mixture. Alternately fold in remaining whites and flour mixture. Gently mix until all ingredients are combined. Bake 12–15 minutes.

While cake is baking, dust a clean cloth with a mixture of the reserved powdered sugar and cocoa. When baking is completed, turn the hot cake out onto the prepared cloth. Remove waxed paper. Trim cake edges. Starting with the long side, tightly roll up the cake with the cloth. Transfer cake, seam side down, to a wire rack to cool.

When cooled, unroll cake and remove cloth. Spread softened ice cream over cake to within ½ inch of the cake edges. Reroll cake. Wrap cake well in plastic wrap and

freeze, seam side down, until firm. When completely frozen, place cake on a serving platter and dust with powdered sugar before slicing and serving. Serve immediately.

TIP: Slices of this cake look divine drizzled with chocolate sauce and garnished with maraschino cherries.

Coconut and Strawberry Sponge Pudding

Yield: 6 servings | **Prep Time:** 10 minutes | **Bake Time:** 30 minutes

The flavor of strawberries and coconut blend nicely together. Consider serving this unusual dessert warm with vanilla ice cream or cool with a generous dollop of sweetened whipped cream.

2 tablespoons butter, softened, plus more to
   butter 6 ramekins
1½ cups strawberries, hulled, halved if
   large, plus more for garnish
¾ cup cream
¾ cup sugar, divided
¼ cup flour
¼ cup shredded sweetened coconut
½ teaspoon salt
3 large eggs, room temperature, separated
½ teaspoon vanilla extract
Boiling water (to sit ramekins in)

Preheat oven to 325° F. Butter 6 ramekins; set aside. In a blender, puree berries and cream; set aside. In a medium bowl, stir ½ cup plus 2 tablespoons sugar, flour, coconut, 2 tablespoons softened butter, and salt in a medium bowl. Stir in egg yolks, berry mixture, and vanilla. In a separate bowl, beat egg whites until foamy. While beating, add remaining 2 tablespoons sugar in a steady stream. Beat until stiff (but not dry) peaks form. Gently fold whites into the strawberry mixture. Ladle batter into the buttered ramekins; place in a large roasting pan. Pour boiling water around the ramekins, halfway up their sides. Bake until golden, about 30 minutes. (If tops brown too quickly, tent with foil strips.) Let cool on a wire rack for 10 minutes. The pudding will set up as it cools.

TIP: A delicious serving idea is to fold finely diced strawberries (½–¾ cup) into sweetened whipped cream and top each ramekin with this mixture.

Pecan Coconut Squares

Yield: 24 squares | **Prep Time:** 15 minutes plus 2 hours for cooling
Bake Time: 5 minutes

Pecans, coconut, and bittersweet chocolate—always a winning combination. This easy dessert is perfect for picnics or parties. Be sure to make lots, because they don't last long!

1 cup butter, at room temperature
¾ cup flour
¾ cup coconut flour (you can also use white flour)
⅓ cup brown sugar, firmly packed
1 14-ounce can sweetened condensed milk
1 14-ounce bag shredded, sweetened coconut
2 teaspoons vanilla extract
1 cup whole pecans
1 12-ounce package bittersweet baking chocolate, roughly chopped (or 12 ounces semisweet chocolate chips)

Preheat oven to 350° F. Line a 9 x 12-inch baking dish with foil so it hangs over the edge (for easy removal and cutting); spray the foil with nonstick cooking spray.

CRUST

In a medium bowl, thoroughly blend butter, flours, and sugar; the mixture should be crumbly. Press crust onto the bottom of the prepared pan, using the back of a measuring cup to create an even layer. Bake for 5 minutes.

FILLING

In a medium bowl, mix the sweetened condensed milk, coconut, and vanilla. Gently spoon the mixture over the baked crust, taking care not to disturb the crust too much. Press pecans gently onto the surface of the coconut mixture.

In the microwave, heat chocolate in glass measuring cup in 30-second increments, stirring in between, until it is just melted. Stir until smooth, but don't over-heat. Chocolate is easy to burn, so you may want to melt it in a small bowl over a pan of simmering water instead. Working

quickly, pour chocolate over the nuts and coconut, spreading it out smoothly. Refrigerate for approximately 2 hours or until firm. When ready to serve, cut into squares.

TIP: If you want the chocolate to spread more easily and evenly, add 1 tablespoon shortening after it has melted; stir to melt the shortening and incorporate it into the chocolate.

Rustic Mixed Berry Tart

Yield: 4 cups filling | **Prep Time:** 20 minutes | **Bake Time:** 30 minutes

A rustic tart is simply a fruit pie made without the pie plate. They're quick and easy to create and the perfect way to start teaching children the fine art of pie making. But the simplicity and ease of this dessert are eclipsed by its beauty and delicious taste. Rustic tarts are an uncommon treat, so next time you need a dessert for a gathering, look no further—this is a winner!

1½ tablespoons fresh lemon juice (from ½ medium to large lemon)
1½ tablespoons cornstarch
2 tablespoons sugar
2 cups fresh raspberries, divided
1½ cups fresh (or frozen) blueberries, divided
1 cup fresh blackberries
1 tablespoon fresh lemon zest
½ recipe Jeanne's No-Fail Pie Crust (page 203)
1 egg white, for basting crust
3 tablespoons turbinado sugar (raw sugar), for sprinkling atop crust and over filling

In a large saucepan, blend lemon juice, cornstarch, and sugar; bring to boil and cook until thickened. Gently fold in 1 cup raspberries, 1 cup blueberries, and the blackberries. Cook 1 more minute, coating fruit with thickened syrup.

Remove from heat. Gently fold remaining berries and lemon zest into cooked fruit.

Preheat oven to 375° F. Roll out prepared crust into large circle or smaller circles, depending on whether you intend to create one large tart or two or three small tarts. Set rolled crust on parchment-lined heavy baking sheet. Place fruit on large circle or divide amongst smaller circles, leaving 2 inches of crust free from fruit filling. Fold the 2 inches of crust up over the filling, creating a rim that encases the filling. Baste crust rim with egg white and sprinkle turbinado sugar over crust rim. Bake approximately 30 minutes or until crust is golden brown.

Cool on wire rack approximately 1 hour then serve with sweetened whipped cream or serve warm with vanilla ice cream.

Neapolitan Bundt Cake

Yield: 12 servings | **Prep Time:** 15 minutes | **Bake Time:** 1 hour

Bundt cakes are a classic dessert—easy to make and pretty to behold. The Neapolitan aspect of this cake, however, adds extra beauty and a fun surprise when slicing into it.

Vanilla Cake Batter

1 cup butter, softened
3 cups sugar
1 cup sour cream
½ teaspoon baking powder
3 cups flour
6 large eggs
1 teaspoon vanilla extract
¼ cup Dutch cocoa
¼ cup milk
¼ cup strawberry jam
3–4 drops red food coloring

Preheat oven to 350° F. Grease a bundt pan well and set aside. In a large bowl, cream butter and sugar. Add sour cream and continue mixing. Add baking powder. Add flour a little at a time, beating until well incorporated. Add eggs, beating in one at a time, and vanilla extract. Divide cake batter into three bowls to prepare 3 separate cake flavors (one bowl for chocolate batter, one for strawberry batter, and one for the existing vanilla batter).

For chocolate cake batter: Beginning with vanilla-flavored cake batter, add ¼ cup Dutch cocoa and ¼ cup milk. Mix well.

For strawberry cake batter: Beginning with vanilla-flavored cake batter, add ¼ cup strawberry jam and 3–4 drops red food coloring.

Using a lever-released ice cream scoop, drop a scoop of vanilla cake batter into the prepared bundt pan. Add a scoop of the strawberry batter next. Then add a scoop of the chocolate batter, all the while encircling the inside of the pan with batters. Repeat this process until all batter has been used.

Bake for 60 minutes or until a toothpick inserted into the center of the cake comes out clean. Let rest on a wire rack for 15 minutes then turn the cake out onto the rack to finish cooling. When cake is completely cooled, glaze with Pink Vanilla Glaze (recipe follows).

PINK VANILLA GLAZE

1½ cups powdered sugar
⅛ teaspoon salt
1 teaspoon butter
¼ teaspoon vanilla extract
2½ teaspoons milk
2–3 drops red food coloring

In a small bowl, mix powdered sugar and salt. In a small microwave-safe bowl, melt butter; mix in vanilla, milk, and food coloring. Add butter mixture to powdered sugar and salt and mix until smooth and creamy. Drizzle glaze over top of bundt cake.

Filled Brownie Squares

Yield: 16 filled squares | **Prep Time:** 40 minutes | **Bake Time:** 20 minutes

This is where a gourmet approach to a proverbial favorite comes into play. While the traditional brownie is one layer that's usually frosted, we created a multi-layered brownie that's exciting to look at and fun to eat!

½ cup melted butter
1 cup sugar
1½ teaspoons vanilla extract
2 large eggs
¼ teaspoon baking powder
½ cup Dutch cocoa powder
½ teaspoon salt
¾ cup flour
Chopped nuts, for garnish (optional)

Preheat oven to 350° F. Cover the interior of an 8 x 8-inch baking pan with a large sheet of foil, large enough so it covers the bottom and extends up and over the pan sides. Spray foil with nonstick cooking spray and coat with sugar.

In a large bowl, blend butter and sugar until creamy. Add vanilla and eggs; stir just until blended. In a separate bowl, mix all dry ingredients. Stir dry ingredients into the butter/sugar mixture. Spoon batter into prepared pan. With wet fingers, spread batter evenly over pan bottom and to all corners. Bake for 20 minutes or until sides pull away from pan and toothpick inserted into middle of pan comes out clean. Cool on wire rack 10 minutes, then use foil handles to carefully lift brownies out of pan; finish cooling on wire rack. Pull foil sides away from brownies to facilitate quicker cooling.

When cool, cut into 16 squares. Slice each square horizontally, creating 32 brownie halves. Frost 16 brownie halves with your favorite frosting—chocolate mint, chocolate peanut butter, and caramel frosting are good choices. Place unfrosted brownie halves atop frosted halves and frost the tops with more frosting. Get creative—each layer could have a different frosting, for instance. Garnish finished brownie stacks with chopped nuts, if desired.

Frozen Lemon Whip

Yield: 8 servings or 1 quart | **Prep Time:** 15 minutes plus freezing time

Lemon desserts are the perfect ending to a meal. Light and refreshing, they complement just about anything they follow and leave folks satisfied without the heavy dessert hangover that commonly results from gooey treats.

1 cup milk (we like to use half-and-half or buttermilk)
1 cup sugar
⅓ cup lemon juice (of course, fresh is best)
1 cup heavy whipping cream
½ teaspoon vanilla extract
1 teaspoon lemon flavoring (lemon emulsion would be superb)

In a small saucepan, heat milk to 175° F; stir in sugar until dissolved. Cool completely. Stir in lemon juice. In a large bowl, beat cream until stiff; fold in vanilla, lemon flavoring, and cooled milk mixture. Pour into a 9-inch square pan. Freeze for 4 hours or until firm, stirring at least once. Remove from the freezer 10 minutes before serving.

NOTE: Lemon zest folded into the cream is a very nice touch to this dessert.

Crème Brûlée

Yield: 6 servings | **Prep Time:** 15 minutes | **Bake Time:** 40 minutes
Cooling Time: 4 hours or longer

Crème Brûlée is like the little black dress. It is simple, elegant, and works for all occasions. A classic finale to a meal, it can be served slightly warm or chilled. And the best news yet? This gourmet-style dessert is easy to make!

6 egg yolks, chilled
6 tablespoons sugar
1½ cups whipping cream
4 cups water
3 tablespoons sugar, for topping

Preheat oven to 275° F. Adjust oven rack to center position. Butter 6 ½-cup custard cups or ramekins and place in a glass baking dish.

In a large bowl, beat egg yolks until slightly thickened. Add sugar and mix until dissolved; mix in cream, then pour mixture into prepared custard cups or ramekins.

In a large saucepan, heat 4 cups of water to simmer. Carefully pour hot water into the glass baking dish; the water should come up to the level of the custard that is inside the cups. This is an important step; the most common mistake people make in baking custard is not surrounding the custard cups with enough water. This step protects your custard from the heat.

Bake approximately 30–40 minutes (25–30 minutes for shallow fluted ramekins), or until custard is set around the edges but still loose in the center. The cooking time will depend largely on the size of the cup or ramekin you are using, but begin checking at 30 minutes and check back regularly after that. When the center of the custard is set, it will jiggle slightly when shaken, and that's when they should be removed from the oven.

Remove from oven and leave in water bath until water has cooled to room temperature. Remove cups from bath, cover with plastic wrap, and refrigerate at least 4 hours.

When ready to serve, uncover custards. If condensation has collected on custards, place paper towel on custard surface to soak up moisture. To create burnt sugar crust, sprinkle 1–2 teaspoons sugar over each crème brulee (tilt and tap cups for even coverage). For best burning results, use a small hand-held torch.

Hold the torch 4–5 inches from the sugar, maintaining a slow and even back-and-forth motion. Stop torching just before the desired degree of doneness is reached, as the sugar will continue to cook for a few seconds after the flame has been removed.

To create a crust without a torch, place brûlées 6 inches below a broiler for 4–6 minutes or until sugar bubbles and turns golden brown. Refrigerate brûlées at least 10 minutes before serving. Serve within 1 hour of torching, as topping will deteriorate.

Cream Cheese Caramel Apple Strata

Yield: 10 servings | **Prep Time:** 15 minutes
Cooling Time: 8 hours or overnight

We created this easy no-bake dessert around a caramel apple theme. It's a decadent show-stopper that gives new meaning to the word gourmet!

1 12.8-ounce package Keebler Sandies® Shortbread cookies, crushed and divided
½ pint *heavy* whipping cream
¼ teaspoon vanilla extract
2 tablespoons powdered sugar
1 8-ounce package cream cheese, softened
1 Granny Smith apple, peeled, pared, and finely chopped
½ cup chopped walnuts (pecans would be lovely as well)
1 14-ounce jar caramel topping, divided

Crush cookies; reserve ½ cup of crumbs to use as garnish. In a medium mixing bowl, combine whipping cream, vanilla, and powdered sugar; whip until stiff peaks form. In a small bowl, mix 2–3 tablespoons of the whipped cream into the softened cream cheese. Gently whip the cream cheese mixture into the whipped cream.

In an 8- or 9-inch square baking pan, spread 1½ cups crushed shortbread cookies. Cover crumbs with 1 cup whipped cream/cream cheese mixture. Layer chopped apple atop cream. Sprinkle chopped nuts over apple layer. Reserve ½ cup caramel topping for garnish; pour remaining topping over apples and nuts. Cover with remaining whipped cream/cream cheese mixture; sprinkle reserved cookie crumbs over cream, and drizzle reserved ½ cup caramel topping over the crumbs and cream. Refrigerate at least 8 hours; overnight is best.

Chocolate Chubbies

Yield: 20 sandwiches | **Prep Time:** 20 minutes | **Bake Time:** 8–10 minutes

Building your own ice cream sandwich is a fun and rewarding treat. Start with this chocolate cookie base and add your favorite ice cream flavor to make a unique and deliciously cooling dessert.

COOKIE

1 cup butter

1½ cups sugar, plus more for sprinkling

1 teaspoon salt

2 large eggs

¼ cup milk, plus more for washing tops of cookies

2 teaspoons vanilla extract

4¼ cups flour, sifted

¾ cup Dutch cocoa powder

1½ teaspoons baking powder

Bring all ingredients to room temperature before beginning. In a large bowl, mix butter, sugar, and salt only enough to combine the ingredients (this results in a chewier cookie). Add eggs, milk, and vanilla; mix only until blended. In a separate bowl, sift flour, cocoa, and baking powder. Add dry ingredients to wet ingredients and mix only until combined.

Preheat oven to 350° F. Prepare baking sheet by oiling it and lining it with parchment or a silicon mat. Transfer dough to a lightly floured surface and roll dough to approximately ⅛ inch thick. Cut out cookies into desired shape (4-inch circles or squares work well) and place on the prepared baking sheet. Using a pastry brush, wash cookie tops with milk and sprinkle with sugar. Bake 8–10 minutes. Do not over-bake—cookies harden as they cool.

ICE CREAM FILLING (for cookie sandwiches)
Prep Time: 40 minutes

1/2 gallon ice cream (your favorite flavor), slightly softened

As cookies cool, spread ½ gallon of softened ice cream ½ to ¾ inches thick on a jelly-roll

pan lined with plastic wrap. Return ice cream to freezer for 20 minutes to harden. Place a baking dish, jelly-roll pan, or cookie sheet in the freezer to chill; this will hold the prepared cookies until they refreeze and will allow for easier individual wrapping of cookies.

When ice cream is hard, remove from freezer and cut out circles or squares slightly smaller than your cookies. Place ice cream cutouts between two cooled cookies and set each sandwich in the baking dish or sheet that you placed in your freezer; work quickly until all cookies are used. Once all cookies are filled, wrap each sandwich individually with plastic wrap and return to the freezer. If no one knows you have these in your freezer, they'll store well for up to 3 months. If the word is out, they'll be gone long before then!

TIP: Having squares of plastic wrap already cut makes wrapping the sandwiches much easier.

Lady Baltimore's Buttermilk Pie
Yield: 6–8 slices | **Prep Time:** 10 minutes | **Bake Time:** 45–50 minutes

While this classic pie has been around for more than fifty years, a new generation of cooks is just now starting to rediscover this simple yet mouth-watering favorite.

3 eggs
1¼ cups sugar
3 tablespoons flour
¼ teaspoon ground nutmeg
1 cup buttermilk
⅓ cup butter, melted
1 teaspoon vanilla extract
1 9-inch unbaked pastry shell

Preheat oven to 400° F. In a large mixing bowl, beat eggs. Add sugar, flour, and nutmeg; mix well. Beat in buttermilk, butter, and vanilla. Pour filling into pastry shell. Bake 10 minutes then reduce oven temperature to 325° F; bake 35–40 more minutes or until a knife inserted in center of pie comes out clean. Cool. To serve, top with berry sauce, fresh fruit, canned fruit filling, or dollops of sweetened whipped cream.

VARIATIONS
Buttermilk Coconut Pie: Add ½ cup flaked unsweetened coconut to the filling.
Buttermilk Pecan Pie: Add 1 cup chopped pecans to the filling.
Buttermilk Lemon Pie: Add 2 tablespoons lemon juice and 1 tablespoon lemon zest to the filling.

Praline Carrot Cake

Yield: 12 servings | **Prep Time:** 40 minutes | **Bake Time:** 40 minutes

Carrot cake is a perennial favorite, but this special version adds a gourmet touch you don't encounter often—a topping of praline icing. While it is delightful without the praline topping, the extra time it takes to make this is so worth the effort. This amazing dessert—layers of moist cake, creamy frosting, indulgent praline sauce, and crunchy pecans—will wow your friends and family with its incredible taste and luscious presentation.

1⅓ cups canola oil

4 eggs

2 cups finely shredded carrots

1 cup crushed pineapple

2 teaspoons vanilla extract

1½ cups chopped pecans (optional, but not on our watch)

⅔ cup shredded coconut (sweetened or unsweetened)

3 cups flour

2 cups sugar

2 teaspoons baking powder

2 teaspoons baking soda

1 teaspoon cinnamon

1 teaspoon salt

Caramel (praline) sauce (recipe follows)

Candied pecans (recipe follows)

Cream cheese frosting (recipe follows)

Preheat oven to 350° F. Butter two 9-inch round cake pans. Combine oil, eggs, carrots, pineapple, vanilla, pecans, and coconut; mix well. Combine and sift dry ingredients; add to the combined moist ingredients. Mix for 2 minutes. Pour batter into prepared cake pans. Bake for 25–30 minutes or until toothpick inserted into middle of cake comes out clean. Turn cake layers onto cooling racks and allow to thoroughly cool.

Place one cooled cake layer on a serving plate. Frost the top of the first layer with cream cheese frosting. Add second layer and frost the outside of the cake with the remaining cream cheese frosting, creating a ¼-inch rim around the perimeter of the top of the cake. (This will help contain the praline sauce.) Cover top of cake with praline sauce and garnish with candied pecans. Store cake in refrigerator until ready to serve.

PRALINE SAUCE

6 tablespoons butter

6 tablespoons brown sugar

¼ cup whipping cream

2 teaspoons vanilla extract

In a small saucepan, melt butter over medium heat. Stir in brown sugar and cream. Cook and stir until mixture comes to a full boil. Reduce heat. Boil gently for 3 minutes, stirring occasionally. Stir in vanilla. Allow to cool.

CANDIED PECANS
¼ cup brown sugar
1 tablespoon orange juice
1 cup pecan halves

Preheat oven to 350° F. Lightly oil a baking sheet. In a small bowl, combine brown sugar and orange juice. Add pecans, stirring to coat. Spread on prepared sheet. Bake 12 minutes or until nuts are browned and syrup is bubbly. Pour nuts onto a sheet of well-buttered waxed paper, separating nuts into single pieces. Allow to cool.

CREAM CHEESE FROSTING
1 8-ounce package cream cheese
½ cup butter
1 teaspoon vanilla extract
6 cups powdered sugar

In a large bowl, beat cream cheese, butter, and vanilla on low until fluffy. Add sugar and beat until frosting is light and smooth.

NO-Fried Ice Cream
Yield: 8 servings | **Prep Time:** 15 minutes | **Freezing Time:** 2–3 hours

What could be more inviting or easier than a fried ice cream that doesn't need frying? Impossible, you say? Read on for how to pull off this delightful slick trick!

6 cups sugar-coated corn flakes, crushed
3 tablespoons melted butter
5 tablespoons corn syrup
2 teaspoons cinnamon
½ gallon vanilla ice cream

In a large bowl, combine crushed cereal, butter, corn syrup, and cinnamon. Shape ice cream into 3-inch balls and roll each in cereal mixture. Press cereal lightly into ball. Place balls in muffin tins and freeze until ready to serve. These are great when placed in a dessert dish and topped with caramel syrup and whipped cream. A fun serving variation is to insert a candy-apple stick into the center of each ball.

Raspberry Custard Tart

Yield: 4 servings | **Prep Time:** 52 minutes plus 2 hours chill time
Bake Time: 25 minutes

This easy and versatile dessert can be made as one 9- or 10-inch tart or 4 individual tarts.

SUGAR COOKIE CRUST

½ cup sugar
½ cup butter, softened to room temperature
1¼ cups flour
¼ teaspoon salt
2 tablespoons milk
1 teaspoon vanilla extract

Preheat oven to 375° F. In a large bowl, cream sugar and butter until light. Add flour, salt, milk, and vanilla; beat until mixture is moist and crumbly (it should clump together when pressed between fingers). Place dough into a 9- or 10-inch tart pan and press it evenly across the bottom and up the sides.

To use with a no-bake filling: Bake 25 minutes or until crust is golden. Cool.

To use with a baked filling: Fill with desired filling and bake for 25 minutes or until crust edges are golden.

HOMEMADE VANILLA CUSTARD
Prep Time: 22 minutes | **Cooking Time:** 20 minutes

½ cup sugar
3 tablespoons cornstarch
½ teaspoon salt
4 egg yolks
3 cups milk
2 tablespoons butter
2½ teaspoons vanilla extract

In a heavy saucepan, bring sugar, cornstarch, salt, egg yolks, and milk to a boil over medium heat (approximately 20 minutes), whisking constantly. The mixture will thicken more as it cools.
Remove from heat and transfer to a medium bowl; add butter and vanilla. Stir well. Place plastic wrap directly on surface of custard to prevent "skin" from forming. Chill 2 hours, removing plastic and stirring occasionally. When custard mixture is completely cooled, spoon into sugar cookie crust.

RASPBERRY WHIPPED CREAM

½ cup fresh raspberries
2 tablespoons powdered sugar
1 cup heavy cream, chilled well

Mash raspberries lightly with a fork until saucy but still chunky. In a medium bowl, whip cream and powdered sugar to form stiff peaks. Gently fold mashed raspberries into whipped cream. Spoon or pipe whipped cream on top of custard.

Chocolate Cherry Bomb Cupcakes

Yield: 24 cupcakes | **Prep Time:** 25 minutes | **Bake Time:** 20 minutes

"The bomb"—that's what we call these culinary delights. They're beautiful to look at and as good as the name implies!

1 Devil's food cake mix
2 3.9-ounce packages instant vanilla
  pudding mix
½ cup sour cream
½ cup canola oil
⅓ cup water
4 eggs
1 teaspoon vanilla extract
½ cup grated dark chocolate (optional)
24 cherry cordials (chocolate-covered cherries)

Preheat oven to 350° F. In a large bowl, blend all ingredients except the cherry cordials. Line two muffin tins with paper cupcake liners. Fill each ⅔ full with batter. Bake for 20 minutes. Let cupcakes cool for 5 minutes. Using a large cake frosting tip, create a space in the center of each cupcake. Push a cherry cordial into this opening. Set cupcakes aside while making Cherry Bomb Cupcake Ganache (recipe follows).

CHERRY BOMB CUPCAKE GANACHE

1 cup sugar
¼ cup milk
½ cup butter
½ cup semi-sweet chocolate chips

In a medium saucepan over medium heat, bring sugar, milk, and butter to a boil. Remove from heat. Add chocolate and stir until melted. Let cool for 5 minutes.

Dip tops of cupcakes into ganache. Remove quickly and allow ganache to cool and harden. Set cupcakes aside while making the Cherry Bomb Cupcake Whipped Topping.

CHERRY BOMB CUPCAKE WHIPPED TOPPING

2 cups heavy cream
1 teaspoon vanilla extract
¼ cup powdered sugar

Whip cream, vanilla, and powdered sugar with an electric mixer until cream holds its shape. Place cream into a pastry bag or plastic zip-top bag with a small piece of the corner cut off; pipe cream onto cupcakes.

Caramel Apple Cheesecake Bites

Yield: 16 servings | **Prep Time:** 30 minutes | **Bake Time:** 40–45 minutes

Another variation on that favorite, the caramel apple, these petite baked treats will satisfy the most discriminating sweet tooth!

CRUST
2 cups flour
½ cup firmly packed brown sugar
1 cup butter, softened

CHEESECAKE FILLING
3 8-ounce packages cream cheese, softened
¾ cup sugar plus 2 tablespoons, divided
3 large eggs
2 teaspoons vanilla extract

APPLES
3 Granny Smith apples, peeled, cored, and
    finely chopped
½ teaspoon cinnamon
¼ teaspoon ground nutmeg

STREUSEL TOPPING
1 cup firmly packed brown sugar
½ cup flour
½ cup whole-wheat flour
½ cup quick-cooking oats
½ cup butter, softened

½ cup walnuts, chopped
½ cup caramel topping

To make crust: Preheat oven to 350° F. In a medium bowl, combine flour and brown sugar. Cut in butter with pastry blender until mixture is crumbly. Press evenly into a 9 x 13-inch baking pan lined with aluminum foil. Bake 15 minutes or until crust is lightly browned.

While crust is baking, place cream cheese and ¾ cup sugar in a large bowl and blend until smooth. Add eggs, one at a time; add vanilla. Stir to combine. Pour filling over warm crust.

In a small bowl, combine chopped apples, remaining 2 tablespoons of sugar, cinnamon, and nutmeg. Spoon evenly over cream cheese mixture.

To make Streusel Topping: In a medium bowl, combine brown sugar, flours, oats, butter, and walnuts. Thoroughly work

butter through the mixture. Sprinkle over apples. Bake for 40–45 minutes, or until filling is set. Remove from oven and drizzle with caramel topping; let cool. Lift baked cheesecake out of pan onto a cutting board; pull foil away from sides of cheesecake. Using a sharp chef's knife, cut cheesecake into 2-inch square bites. These are yummy eaten out of hand but also make a lovely presentation when arranged on a pretty serving tray with a dollop of sweetened whipped cream placed atop each square.

Lime Ricky Cupcakes

Yield: 12 servings | **Prep Time:** 40 minutes | **Bake Time:** 20 minutes

A basic white cupcake flavored with a lime glaze drizzle and topped with a luscious cream cheese frosting—decadent is what this cupcake is all about.

CUPCAKES

½ cup butter, room temperature
1¼ cups sugar
2 large eggs
3 tablespoons fresh lime juice
Zest from one lime
¼ teaspoon neon-green food coloring
1⅓ cups flour
1½ teaspoons baking powder
1¼ teaspoons baking soda
¼ teaspoon salt
¾ cup buttermilk

Preheat oven to 350° F. Line a standard muffin tin with 12 cupcake liners. In a medium bowl, beat butter and sugar until smooth. Beat in eggs one at a time; add lime juice, lime zest, and food coloring. In a medium bowl, sift dry ingredients; alternately beat flour mixture and buttermilk into the lime mixture. Spoon ⅓ cup batter into each cupcake liner. Bake for 20 minutes or until a toothpick inserted in the center of a cupcake comes out clean. Cool 10 minutes and remove cupcakes from pan.

GLAZE DRIZZLE

1 cup powdered sugar
2½ tablespoons lime juice

In a small bowl, combine powdered sugar and lime juice until smooth.

While cupcakes are still warm, use a toothpick to poke small holes into each cupcake. When cupcakes are completely cooled, drizzle with glaze, coating tops well. Frost with frosting (recipe follows).

FROSTING

1 8-ounce package cream cheese, softened
1½ cups powdered sugar
½ cup butter, softened
1 tablespoon finely grated lime peel
1 teaspoon vanilla extract

Beat all ingredients until smooth and creamy. Frost cupcakes.

52 Tips for Cooking Smarter

Human nature being what it is, we tend to do things that are easiest. So it makes sense that if we create easier ways to do things, we're likely to do them more often. In that spirit, here are 52 tips (one for every week of the year) to consider and try. We've turned these well-tested ideas into habits and find they save us lots of time and energy as we work in the kitchen.

1. Plan, plan, plan. Creating a weekly menu is a great way to keep your kitchen time—and your wallet—on track. You'll also reduce the number of trips to the grocery store! Notice how long your cooking will take for each meal and plan accordingly. Another good tip is to spend some time prepping foods for the week on Saturday.

2. Partner with ice cube trays—they're your friends. Pesto, broths and stocks, some soups, marinara sauce, and even citrus juice freeze really well and last for quite a while. Just move the cubes to plastic freezer bags once they're fully frozen.

3. Know how to use your knives. Does it take you forever to chop up garlic? Does it seem like you spend more time cutting veggies than you do actually cooking? The problem could be that you're not handling your knives properly or that you're using the wrong type of knife for the job.

4. Make meals—or parts of meals—in advance. Soups, casseroles, and quiches are all tasty foods that still taste great a few days later. You can also make sauces, dressings, and other recipe components in advance.

5. Preheat the oven. Putting food in an oven that hasn't been fully preheated causes your meal to be unevenly cooked and increases the time it's in the oven. Preheating lets you cut down on cooking time.

6. Prep everything before cooking. Don't wait until the lasagna's almost out of the oven to grate the cheese you need for garnishing. Chop all your veggies before you start cooking. It's amazing how much time can be saved by not going back and forth between prepping and cooking.

7. Make note of the time it takes to prepare various things. So many recipes have an estimated prep and cooking time, yet don't exactly line up with how long it actually takes. Time yourself and make note of how long it takes to fix your favorite recipes.

8. Clean while you're cooking. Mom's favorite tip: Don't leave all the cleanup for after the meal! Keep a sink full of sudsy water and wash pots, pans, utensils, and other items as you go.

9. Skip shredding cheese one recipe at a time—just do it all in advance! An expensive time-saver, shredded cheese is pricier than a cheese block. So buy a block and shred the entire block yourself. Then freeze all but what you need for the week—cheese freezes well. You'll save time and money!

10. Mix dried herbs and spices in advance. You love that perfect mix of parsley, sage, rosemary, and thyme for so many of your recipes! Make a batch in advance, label it, and store it in an airtight container.

11. Move your garbage can to your prep station or tape a plastic bag to your counter where you're prepping. You'll save steps by not running back and forth to the garbage can.

12. Make your own snacks in advance. Love trail mix, granola, or other tasty snacks? Mix them up and portion them out once a week. You'll save loads of time and always be prepared for your 2 P.M. snack break.

13. Mix liquids (whipping cream, pudding, gravy, and others) **in a paper bag that you put in your sink.** Place your bowl of ingredients in the bottom of the bag and reach in with your electric mixer. All the splatters will land on the insides of the bag instead of on your backsplash, counter appliances, or underneath the upper cupboards. It's a real time-saver if you can avoid splatters and the cleanup they involve. (There's another advantage: Placing the bag in the sink creates an ergonomically correct position for mixing—no hunching your shoulder as you mix.)

14. Don't run to the store when you run out of staples. Make your own brown sugar, baking powder, buttermilk, powdered sugar, oat flour, and other staples. You'll find plenty of recipes for these on the Internet.

15. Keep your pantry stocked using an ongoing inventory list to avoid running out of things.

16. Keep staple ingredients (those you use often) within arm's reach. For instance, indispensable baking supplies might be baking powder; baking soda; cornstarch; cornmeal; extracts, such as vanilla and almond; baking cocoa; honey; molasses; granulated, powdered, and brown sugar; cooking oil and shortening; and dry yeast.

Useful baking ingredients could include cake and cookie decorations; chocolate chips and other baking chocolates; shredded coconut; and sweetened condensed milk.

Indispensable condiments might include ketchup; mayonnaise; mustard; salad dressing; soy and steak sauces; cider, white, balsamic, red, and white wine vinegar; and Worcestershire sauce.

Then there are indispensable freezer staples. These might include fruit juice concentrates; piecrusts; and frozen vegetables, such as carrots, spinach, whole-kernel corn, broccoli, cauliflower, and peas.

A few useful freezer staples could be bread and pizza doughs, pesto sauce, phyllo dough, and puff pastry.

In the grain, pasta, and bread department, there are also some indispensables. These might include bread and Panko crumbs; cornmeal; crackers; various pastas, such as spaghetti, rotini, shells, fettuccini, lasagna, egg noodles, and elbow macaroni; rice; oatmeal; and stuffing mix. Other useful items in this category could include barley, couscous, quinoa, kasha, tortillas, and wild rice.

Finally, there are some indispensables found in cans, bottles, and bags that are always smart to have on hand. These might include tomato products, such as juice, paste, sauce, sun-dried, and stewed; bouillon cubes or granules; broth; canned fruit and applesauce; dried fruit; canned, dried, and bagged beans; soups; canned and dried mushrooms; olives; gelatins; nuts; olive and sesame oil; peanut butter; pie fillings;

jams and preserves; salts; and tuna. Other useful items in this category could include artichoke hearts, bamboo shoots, chilies, clams, salmon, pimientos, and roasted red peppers.

17. Keep on hand and always use "gravel."
Gravel is a freezer-prepped ingredient you make ahead and freeze. Good candidates for preparing ahead and freezing for later use are: cooked ground beef and sausage; chopped celery, bell peppers, and onions; and grated cheeses.

To prepare: After food is cooked, chopped, and grated, spread it out in thin layers on large jelly roll pans or cookie sheets. Cover the sheets with plastic wrap and place them in the freezer. These foods will freeze in 2–3 hours; however, if you get busy and forget them, there's no harm done. After the food is frozen, break it up and store it in labeled, zip-top freezer bags or plastic freezer containers in proportions you use in your favorite recipes.

Suggestions for using "gravel":
- Sloppy Joes
- Tacos, tostados, and enchiladas
- Soups and stews
- Stroganoff gravy
- Calzones and pizzas
- Marinara sauces
- Hot sandwiches

18. **When not using them, store your oversized grilling tools in a sealed plastic bag either hung from the grill or on the grill with the lid down.** This habit saves precious space in your kitchen and keeps your tools where you use them.

19. **Separate your cooking herbs from your baking spices and store them separated from each other.** This will save you time when hunting for ingredients—you won't be pawing through things you don't need at the moment for the few you do need right then.

20. **Try this for the fastest way to pit olives:** Put the olives on a cutting board, whack them with the broad side of a chef's knife, and lift out the pits.

21. **If you don't have time to chill a stew or stock before skimming off the fat, try this quick and easy method:** Fill a heavy plastic bag halfway with ice cubes, seal, and set in the freezer. When the stew has cooled, drag the bag across the surface of your stew or stock then lift it out. The fat will harden on the ice-cold bag. Rinse and repeat until all the fat has been removed.

22. **How to seed a pepper quickly:** Put the pepper on its side and, using a sharp utility knife, slice off a small portion of the bottom. Stand the pepper upright. Repeat three times, turning the pepper a quarter turn each time. You'll be left with 4 large clean slices of pepper—the seeds will remain attached to the core.

23. **To remove seeds quickly from a squash, use a melon baller.** Cut the squash in half lengthwise, then run the baller down the seeds, scooping them out.

24. **Crying when chopping onions slows down the process, so avoid those tears!** Pour a little white vinegar on your chopping board before chopping your onions. It'll absorb the fumes. For double protection, burn a candle as you work. The flame will neutralize the fumes. Or try chopping Grandma's way—with a slice of bread between your lips.

25. **Shortcut prep time by making basic mixes ahead.** Muffin and biscuit mixes are the perfect example. There are lots of great recipes for make-ahead mixes on the Internet.

26. **Save baking time by using rapid-rise yeast.** You'll avoid the wait that "proofing" takes. Simply follow package directions.

27. **When you're making bread dough, make an extra batch and freeze it for future use.** After kneading the dough, shape it into a disk. Place in a self-sealing plastic bag and freeze for up to 1 month. When you're ready to bake, thaw the dough in the bag in the refrigerator for 8–16 hours or on the countertop for 4–9 hours.

28. **Avoid the unnecessary cleanup and waste that weevil create by keeping all flour refrigerated or frozen.** Another trick is to store flour in ½-gallon canning jars with the lids screwed on tightly. Grain products attract bugs, so always move them from the grocery store packaging they come in to glass or metal containers with tight lids.

29. **Save time when making lasagna by not pre-cooking your noodles.** Just increase the amount of tomato sauce, tomato paste, or marinara and layer your dish with uncooked noodles. Bake the lasagna covered with foil, and the noodles will absorb all the liquid they need to be perfectly *al dente*. Also, if you make your lasagna the day before you plan to bake and serve it, the noodles will absorb liquid while sitting in the refrigerator.

30. **Want to save hundreds of hours over the course of a year during cooking?** Learn to use a pressure cooker. Busy and experienced cooks all say they can't live without their pressure cooker.

31. **Save kitchen space and cleanup time by ditching your electric veggie steamer and** **opting for an inexpensive, easy-to-store, expandable stainless-steel steamer.** It can be opened to fit just about any size pot and it's so much easier to clean than an electric steamer.

32. **When it's the season to can or freeze corn, save time by scalding your ears of corn in your dishwasher.** Pre-clean the washer with a vinegar rinse. Remove the husks and silk, then stand the ears upright on the top rack and lay them horizontally on the bottom rack. Set the temperature of your hot water heater as high as it will go then set your dishwasher on the rinse cycle. Lots of corn gets scalded simultaneously!

33. **Save time and minimize kitchen cleanup by canning fruit on a camp stove on your deck or patio.** Don't do this on a cool or breezy day, however. Scalding-hot jars lifted from their boiling water bath can crack if a cool breeze hits them.

34. **Save on baking time and avoid the risk of wasting ingredients by making sure your oven is the right temperature.** We've spoiled a lot of good food because our ovens weren't accurate. A good oven thermometer can tell you how "right on" or how "far off" your oven is so you can adjust temperatures for baking.

35. **If you're in a hurry and don't have time to make a glaze, just use marmalade**

or fruit jelly to glaze beets, carrots, winter squash, or parsnips. Just add a couple of tablespoons of either marmalade or jelly and some butter to your hot vegetables; toss until everything glistens.

36. **When you're running late and would rather not take the time to chop or mince garlic, just rub the inside of your baking dish with a cut garlic clove instead.** Allow enough time for the garlic juice to dry before buttering the dish. This technique works really well if only a hint of garlic will suffice.

37. **Save time and energy when marinating.** The easiest way to marinate meat for any recipe is to put both the meat and the marinade in a heavy self-sealing plastic bag. It makes it easy to move the meat around to coat it with marinade, it takes up little space in the refrigerator, and it requires no cleanup.

38. **Collect easy and quick meal recipes and use them in your menu every week. When children are old enough, assign them their own quick and easy recipe to practice; assign them a certain night of the week to prepare "their" recipe for family dinner.** By delegating some of the cooking and cleanup, you'll save a tremendous amount of time and energy throughout the year.

39. **Save time and frustration when peeling hard-cooked eggs.** You'll have the easiest time if you crack the wide end of the shells and plunge the eggs into ice water the moment they are drained from the cooking water. A quick chill in ice water also helps to keep the gray-green ring from forming between the yolk and white. When the eggs are cool, craze the shell by tapping it gently. This allows you to pull away the thin membrane that surrounds the egg when you peel off the shell. If the membrane sticks to the egg white, it will not peel neatly. Ask us how we know this!

40. **Save time when rolling pie crusts.** Rather than flouring your work surface, lay out a large square of plastic wrap (made by overlapping two long strips to form a square). Place pie crust ball in the middle of the plastic wrap, cover with another large square of plastic wrap, and roll as usual.

When ready to place crust in pie pan, simply remove top plastic, slip your hand under the bottom plastic and flip crust into pie pan.

If a top crust is needed, repeat the process. This technique saves you from the hassle of cleaning up the typical flour mess left behind on the counter.

41. **Save time and money by stocking up on marked-down angel food cakes.**

Angel food cake freezes beautifully. Simply put it in a plastic bag, squeeze out as much air as possible, seal, and freeze for up to 3 months. A thawed cake can be used to make fresh fruit trifle, can be covered with your favorite frosting, or can be used as a good replacement for the shortcake when serving fresh berries and sweetened whipped cream.

42. Don't waste time scraping tomato paste out of that little can or scraping cream of whatever soup out of its can. Instead, after you remove one end of the can, tip it over (nothing will spill) and punch a hole in the other end with a sharp, sturdy knife. This releases the vacuum, and the can contents will slide right out—no muss, no fuss.

43. When cleaning up after dinner, have a consistent routine. This time- and energy-saving routine has been at work in our homes for years. First decide if you want diners to carry their dirty dishes to the kitchen (this can create more work than it's worth, so think this through). If you do follow this practice, ask each person who is tall enough to reach the faucet to rinse and stack his or her dishes on a counter area designated for this purpose. Next carry all food from table to the countertop and place leftovers in appropriate-size containers. Place prepared food in the refrigerator.

Fill the sink with sudsy hot water; place all dishes, pans, or utensils that you don't want in the dishwasher in the sudsy sink. Allow these items to soak while you load the dishwasher with all items that have been rinsed. Then wipe down the table, countertops, and stove top. Finally, wash and dry items in the sink. Wipe down the refrigerator door and sweep the floor. Voila! Your kitchen is now clean and ready for its next tour of duty. Of course, every one of these steps can and should be delegated. The best time-saver of all is delegation.

44. Save time chopping salad greens and other vegetables. Place items in a large wide-bottomed bowl and run a pizza slicer back and forth a few times through your greens.

45. When it's time to move, save time packing your plates. Rather than packing plates individually in newspaper, place plates in between inexpensive paper plates. Then wrap the entire stack in several layers of newspaper.

46. Save time and energy by using your nutcracker to twist off a stuck cap. The gadget lends extra gripping power when you're dealing with stubborn soda bottle caps as well.

47. **Use newspaper to ripen tomatoes faster.** Wrap each tomato in newspaper and leave it out at room temperature. Check them often because the process happens fairly quickly.

48. **Save time and hassle when slicing soft cheese, cheesecake, or hard-cooked eggs.** Wrap a piece of dental floss tightly around one finger of each hand, hold firmly, and press down.

49. **Save on prep time when crumbling hard-cooked eggs.** Use a mesh strainer—just push a few eggs at a time through the mesh. You'll be done in no time.

50. **Save time by not checking the water level in your double boiler.** Add a few marbles to the bottom pan; the marbles will rattle when the water level gets low. When you hear the rattle, you know for sure it's time to add more water or remove the pan from the heat.

51. **You'll have less mess and after-meal cleanup if you use a lettuce leaf to contain taco fillings.** Line each shell with a lettuce leaf before ladling in meat and toppings.

52. **Save cleanup time when carving meat and poultry.** Place your entrée on a jelly-roll pan. All juices and carving remnants will fall into the pan rather than onto your counter top. For cleanup, simply rinse the pan and place it in the dishwasher.

About the Authors

Jeanne Mae Wolfley is a former cooking and nutrition online newsletter researcher and contributor. She co-edited the cooking magazine *Cook'n* and is co-author of the daily blog, "Dinner Our" (it's "Our Dinner" backwards!). Jeanne grew up in Port Angeles, Washington; married her high school sweetheart, Ross S. Wolfley; and has lived all over the western United States and England because of Ross's service as a USAF fighter pilot. This gave her an opportunity to learn cooking skills and tips from many parts of the world. When Jeanne is not writing and cooking, she loves to spend time with her five children and their spouses, whom she adores almost as much as her eighteen grandchildren. Home is where her heart is, and she enjoys taking classes, sewing, reading, and painting. Jeanne loves to cook for family and friends and learned many of her skills from her mother, Mae Sandum, who was a professional cook. If there's a neighborhood gathering where food is involved, Jeanne's recipes are the ones folks eagerly turn to! Visit Jeanne at www.dinnerour.blogspot.com and www.everydaygourmet.com.

Kaycee Leishman has worked in commercial photography for seven years. She is the photographer for the national crafting and scrapbooking magazine *CRICUT* and is the former photographer for the cooking magazine *Cook'n*. Kaycee attended her first photography class when she was twelve years old and knew she was in love. The old adage, "An image is worth a thousand words," truly became her impetus. Hundreds of rolls of film and years later, Kaycee earned her bachelor's degree in photography from Brigham Young University. Following graduation she worked for several years in wedding and portrait photography until she found her true calling shooting still-life subjects (she found still-life to be more cooperative than mothers of the bride). Kaycee now lives in Utah with her husband and three boys, who enjoy taste-testing the subjects of her still-life work. If she's not shooting mouth-watering photographs, you'll find Kaycee chasing her boys around the house, singing songs of her own creation, or out running. Kaycee regularly contributes to the cooking website www.everydaygourmet.com.

Alice Osborne, coordinator for Community and Continuing Education at Utah Valley University, co-authored a bestselling book on clutter, *It's Here . . . Somewhere*, and co-edited the cooking magazine *Cook'n*. Alice contributes to a weekly cooking and nutrition online newsletter and is co-author of the daily blog, "Dinner Our" ("Our Dinner" backwards!). Raised in Spokane, Washington, Alice learned at an early age how much she loved organizing and cooking. While her little girlfriends were "playing" house, Alice was "organizing" the house— rearranging the silverware drawer, tidying up the linen closet, moving her bedroom furniture around—and experimenting with her mother's recipes. Growing up under tough economic circumstances, Alice discovered she had a flair for making the best of her circumstances— something she still practices with relish. This early training served her well as she raised her seven children in tiny square footage minus a dishwasher, extra bathrooms, or even a grocery budget. Alice's background of creatively "making do" is the wellspring of ideas for her writing and shows up in the organization and cooking classes she teaches. And if there's anything she loves as much as her family, it would be helping folks de-clutter and learn to cook creatively so they can make the best of *their* circumstances! Visit Alice at www.dinnerour.blogspot.com and www.everydaygourmet.com.

Index

F

G

H

W

Waffle syrups, 52
Waffles, Norwegian, 57
Watermelon and crab Napoleans, 132
Weekly menu, creating, 238
Weevil, how to avoid, 242
Wendell's Maple Bars and Glazed
      Doughnuts, 38
Whip, frozen lemon, 217
Whipped cream, raspberry, 231
White bean and tuna sandwich, 73
White chocolate macadamia nut muffins, 30
Wild rice and chicken soup, 185
Wraps, chicken and lettuce, 12

Y

Yeast, rapid-rise, 241
Yellow Squash Casserole, 171
Yogurt and dill dip, 15

Z

Zesty Garden Salsa, 11
Zucchini Cheese Soup, 194
Zucchini Gratin, 172